Walking in the Spirit in
COLOMBIA
A Matter of Life or Death

Chadwick
Martin
Stendal

2002

Walking in the Spirit in Colombia

A Matter of Life or Death

by

Chadwick M. Stendal

Art work by Osvaldo and Diana Lara
Layout by Marta Jaramillo R.

ISBN 0-931221-49-8

Bible quotations are from the King James or the New King
James Versions.

Colombia para Cristo   Ransom Press Int'l
P.O. Box 400   Apartado Aereo 95.300
Moore Haven, FL 33471   Bogota, Colombia
USA   SOUTH AMERICA
patstendal@aol.com

Printed in Colombia

Table of Contents

I want to dedicate this book to my wife,

Pat

Her adaptation to primitive living with four small children could only have been accomplished by the love of God being shed abroad in her heart through the Holy Spirit. She was an unlikely candidate for a pioneer missionary. On our first trip over the border to Mexico on vacation from my engineering job, she went into severe culture shock only the second day and lay on the bed, unable to get up, exclaiming, "If only I could have a hamburger and a malted milk."

When I found her some milk and cheese that said 'pasteurized' and a sealed loaf of bread, she sat up and made a sandwich and felt much better. Then I made the mistake of driving her past the store where I bought the food, and when she saw the four sides of beef hanging out in front covered with flies and turning green, she almost lost her lunch. How the Lord called her to the mission field with a special call will be covered in her coming new book.

She has a genuine love for both the Indians and the Spanish- speaking Colombians, living for a great many years in the most primitive conditions, sometimes cooking on the ground with firewood and doing the family laundry in the river. Her daily tender loving care for the malnourished, parasite ridden Indians gave sick Indians the will to live. One old lady said when Pat had walked for hours in the deep mud to get to where she was dying, "Look how much she loves me." She immediately asked for food and started to recover.

Pat's smiling face and loving kindness so amazed the Kogis that they wanted me to give them pills to make their ornery wives act nicer. When I said there were no such pills, one Kogi man said, "We have been watching you carefully, but we can't discover when you hit your wife with a piece of firewood, because everyone knows that women do not attend to all their duties without being regularly beaten.

I sensed an opportunity to present the 'Good News.' I told them that Pat was not always so nice and helpful but that God had changed her life, and that He could transform their lives and their spouses lives as well. One man was very thoughtful as he contemplated this revolutionary new thought. Then he replied, "I suppose it's possible for God to change a man's life, but a woman, <u>never</u>!

However, nothing is too hard for our God, and now there are Kogi women with transformed lives.

Chapter I

The Reality of the Spiritual Realm

I was working as a young engineer in Grand Rapids, Minnesota and the Lord was working with me to draw me into a close relationship with Himself. One night I had a very vivid and prophetic dream.

In my dream I entered the house and found that the light switch didn't work. Then someone grabbed me violently from behind. I fought him off in the dark and groped my way to the bedroom where I had a pistol in a drawer by the bed. I became terrified to find the gun gone, and I could hear my assailant ramshakling the house looking for me.

I managed to get to the kitchen in an attempt to find a knife or something with which to defend myself. The knives were all gone, and all I could find was an old fashioned can opener with a small ¼ inch point on it. I found a small flashlight and opened a small closet where I kept a rifle. The rifle was gone, but my wide-brimmed hat that I wore around town was there. It was slashed into small pieces with a knife. With horror I realized that my assailant hated me so much that just the sight of my hat put him into an angry frenzy.

Finally I remembered that I had a shotgun in the basement at the foot of the stairs. I found the door to the basement and quickly descended the stairs, frantic to get a hold of the shotgun. It was not there. Just then the door at the head of the stairs opened, and a big powerful man thumped down the stairs with a big flashlight in his hands. There was nowhere to hide.

I woke up trembling uncontrollably. I reached for my pistol from the drawer by the side of the bed. I sat up for some time in the bed with my pistol still in my hands, still shaking. Two Bible verses went through my mind. . . . *Your adversary the devil walks about like a roaring lion, seeking whom he may devour.* I Peter 5:8 and . . . *Satan has asked for you, that he may sift you as wheat, but I have prayed for you, that your faith fail not.* Luke 22:31, 32. What was happening was that as I drew closer to the Lord, I was becoming a threat to Satan, and the Lord was giving me a warning.

I can always tell when I am walking especially close to the Lord. First I start to experience very strong opposition from Satan, rumors, lies, and opposition of all kinds. Often the opposition comes from other Christians and Christian leaders. This opposition is overcome through prayer and resisting the devil. *Resist the devil and he will flee from you.* James 4:7

When I was eighteen, I turned everything I owned over to the Lord, according to the Gospels. *If anyone desires to come after Me, let him deny himself, and take up his cross, and follow Me.* Matt. 16:24. For several years I walked in victory in the army, and it wasn't until I was back home again and joined a church that I started downhill due to the lukewarm attitude of the members. I attended that church until I was 28, and then I became dissatisfied with the lukewarm life I was leading. After a crisis experience, the Lord showed me what it meant to *'walk in the Spirit.'* Gal. 5:16 All my decisions, small and great, had to have the Lord's direction. I moved into a whole new dimension of intimate relationship with the Lord. This relationship brought about a life of victory through listening to the Lord's voice and trusting Him for victory. *My sheep hear My voice, and I know them, and they follow Me.* John 10:27

I thought that the pastor and elders of the evangelical church I was attending would be pleased that I was learning to walk in the Spirit and hear the Lord's voice. Instead they got extremely angry and said that in this dispensation, God does not speak to individuals except through the Scriptures. Therefore if I was hearing anything in the spirit, it had to be from the devil.

There were six others in the church that God was speaking to, and finally on Mother's Day with the church full of people, the pastor began a diatribe against these terrible people in the church who were guilty of multiple sins and were treading the Scriptures underfoot. I rose to my feet and said, "Pastor, if you have anything against anyone you are supposed to go to him privately, and if he will not receive you, try again with witnesses, and finally bring it before the church. You have brought this matter directly to the church without talking it over with me."

At this point the pastor said, "Somebody throw that man out of the church. Two angry men came to where Patty and I were sitting and started pushing us toward the door. Patty was expecting, and as they began jostling and shoving Patty, I almost lost my cool. As they shoved us down the outside steps, I remember calling back, "We really love you all."

This incident caused me great mental anguish. These were my friends. We attended an early morning prayer time and visited the jail together with other church members. Then came the shunning. Nobody from the church would speak to me or greet me on the street. I would say, "Hi, brother Dave," and extend my hand. He would ignore me and leave my hand extended in the air. Some people would cross the street when they saw me coming to avoid meeting me. In a small town of about 6,000, this all began to be very disagreeable. They took the view that I was of the devil and justified these actions on that basis.

Meanwhile the Lord was teaching me to walk in the Spirit. I was Project Engineer of the radar station, and a young lieutenant arrived to work on the operation of the station. The Lord gave me just the right words to lead him to the Lord.

The Lord directed me to go to the jail. Normally we went to the jail on Sundays, and the jailor would ask the inmates, "Anyone for church?" Usually a few would respond. I had a huge Bible under my arm, my pockets were loaded with tracts, and lesson one of a Bible correspondence course was in my back pocket. After I recited the six steps to salvation, the prisoner would give me a blank look and say something like, "Have you got 50 cents for a pack of cigarettes?"

But this time directed by the Lord, arriving outside visiting hours, the jailor was very nice to me and brought me a tough-looking young man in a torn T-shirt. I prayed about what to say to him. I realized he was not going to respond to a canned six point soul-winning presentation. The Lord led me to talk about his family. As I spoke about his mother, he broke down and began to tremble and cry. It was not hard to lead him to a full repentance. His facial expression changed from rebellion to joy, as the Lord forgave his sins. He said, "I can hardly wait to call my mother who has been praying for me every day to tell her the good news." There were many more conversions that year as I learned that there is a key to every person's heart that the Holy Spirit can reveal to those who walk in the Spirit. It may take time to win your friend or loved one, but *God is not willing that any should perish, but that all should come to repentance.* II Peter 3:9

I had never before in my Christian life walked close enough to the Lord to be any kind of threat to Satan. The lies and rumors against me got worse. I did not realize how formidable Satan could be, as the worst was yet to come. The next Sunday, a lady friend of ours asked if it was true that I had thrown down the Bible and stomped on it. I said, "No, of course not! Where would you ever get that idea!" It developed that her pastor had attended a meeting of all the pastors of northern Minnesota where the pastor that had thrown me out stated that I had trodden underfoot the Bible. He stated it in such a way that the other pastors took it literally, and some of them denounced me from their pulpits the next Sunday. So now I was getting shunned by even more people.

I went to the pastor who threw me out and said, "Pastor, you know I didn't literally stomp the Bible underfoot. You need to go to these pastors and straighten this thing out."

"I'm not straightening anything out," he responded, "You got it coming." I had considered the pastor a personal friend before the Lord taught me to walk in the Spirit. I couldn't believe that this was happening to me. How could my friends turn on me so viciously? I just wished I could dig a big hole and disappear.

This was the beginning of the Lord teaching me a great spiritual truth. All problems, difficulties, and supposed personal affronts are marvelous opportunities to grow in grace and develop the fruits of the Spirit. We need to look at things from God's viewpoint. He's trying to develop and perfect us, so we can rule and reign with Him, and we are busy complaining about our difficulties. I knew from the Scripture that we are supposed to rejoice and be glad when people say all kinds of evil against us falsely. Matt. 5:12 So I said to my friend, who was thrown out of the church at the same time I was, "We're supposed to rejoice now. The only trouble is, I don't feel like rejoicing."

He replied, "I don't feel like rejoicing either."

Right at this time came a temptation in the form of a fine job offer in another town. I was trying to walk in the Spirit and look to the Lord for all decisions. In my heart, I knew the Lord wanted me to stay in Grand Rapids and face all the enmity and false rumors that were bombarding me, but the job offer was very appealing. It was to be Project Engineer of the Farmington NIKE missile base. It carried with it a promotion and higher pay. Instead of praying it through and getting the Lord's will on applying for the job, which I now know would have been to stay where I was, I decided to put my name in for the job and make the decision to move or not if I was offered the job. After all, there were many engineers in the St. Paul District Corps of Engineers who wanted the job and had more experience than I. The normal procedure would have been for them to send the job offer to me, and then I thought there would be time in which that I could pray about it and accept or reject the offer. Bad idea! The Chief Engineer sent two engineers to replace me, and I was relieved of my job in Grand Rapids.

As I left Grand Rapids for Farmington, I got an icy cold feeling in my heart as I realized I was out of the will of the Lord. The farther I got from Grand Rapids, the colder I became spiritually until I was 'stone cold dead in the market' as I began to lay out the missile base in Farmington.

The Farmington NIKE missile base, just south of Minneapolis and St. Paul, was just the kind of important construction job I had always wanted to head up. All the plans were secret and involved three underground missile storage buildings with huge 55 ft. long hydraulic elevators to bring the missiles to the surface for firing at enemy bombers. It even had an atomic warhead storage building, its own water and electricity, and barracks for 200 men. The electronic security system was supplemented with K-9 guard dogs.

It was a bright summer day without a cloud in the sky when I set up my transit to lay out the first construction lines. As I worked, a little dark cloud came overhead and dropped a drenching rain, totally soaking me and chilling me to the bone. A wind came along, and I was shivering while in the rest of the sky, the sun was shining. I went home and became very sick. I knew I had no ordinary flu. Bloody sputum came up, and I felt terrible. I croaked out to Patty, "Get me a doctor right away."

The doctor came to the house and examined me and took me in his own car directly to the hospital. Soon I was under an oxygen tent as the doctor tried to save my life. He cut out all food of any kind. He later said that the energy lost digesting anything could have been enough to kill me. Under the oxygen tent, I realized I was dying as the antibiotics hadn't kicked in yet, and I didn't know if they would before I died. I was only 28 years old, and I couldn't believe my life was ending. I knew exactly why I was there. I said, "Lord, give me another chance. I'll go back to Grand Rapids even if I have to sweep floors for a living. I was totally serious. As soon as I made this decision, I began to recover.

A funny thing happened. Some kind of centennial was being celebrated in Grand Rapids at the time I left so suddenly, and many of the men wore beards, including me. Beards were extremely rare in those days, and people said to me, "You're not going into the Twin Cities area with that outlandish beard, are you?"

I said, "Yes, I am. I want all the people on my new job to think, 'The new engineer on the job chews nails.'" I was trying to make everybody believe I was no one to fool with and project more maturity than my 28 years would indicate. Nurses in the hospital would come to the door of my room to see the bearded engineer from the north woods. My first meal after I started to recover was milk toast. The Lord said to me, "The new engineer on the job eats milk toast." I learned my lesson and shaved off the beard. I realized that the Lord has a keen sense of humor.

When I recovered and started making plans to return to Grand Rapids, the Lord made it clear that I could stay and finish the missile base. He was after obedience and willingness, and once that was established, He was satisfied. My home church was in Bloomington, and I commuted there for services. I continued with the Boys' Brigade, taught Sunday School and sang in the choir. Meanwhile Patty resumed working with the Pioneer Girls and was active in the summer camp program. A trip to Mexico during my vacation made me aware of the tremendous need for missionary work among the large number of poor Indians. One third of the Mexican people are Indians, speaking over 100 dialects.

I became chairman of the missions board of our church. I pushed missions among our young people and planned missions conferences. I secured a high-powered missions speaker from a mission that thought you better have a good reason if you were not on the mission field. When this man arrived at our house, he didn't even explain who he was or greet me. His first words were, "Why aren't you on the mission field?"

This caught me off guard, and I stammered, "Well, I would be, only I don't have any connections." The man looked me in the eye and then looked straight up at the heavens and then said incredulously, "You don't have any connections?" His meaning was clear. What kind of a Christian was I without any connections with God.

I tried to explain that neither my church nor I had any extra funds for missions work. The next Sunday he preached, "The fields are white unto harvest, but the money is short." He told tale after tale of God supplying funds for His work. He told how he had arrived in the Philippians with 10 cents in his pocket, and God supplied all his needs, and he soon had a Bible Institute flourishing. So much for my excuse that I didn't have any finances, as God was beginning to call me to the mission field.

I began reading books on missions and speaking with missionaries on furlough. Naomi Skoglund, a missionary with over 30 years experience, stayed in our home for a few days. I asked her, "Naomi, how were you called to the mission field?" I was not prepared for her answer.

"God called me with an audible voice, just like Samuel." God called, "Naomi! Naomi!"

She said, "What is it, Lord?"

God said, "I want you to go to Africa as a missionary!"

Naomi said, "Lord, I don't have any talents. Send my sister who is musical and has many abilities."

God said, "I am not interested in special abilities. I want you to go, and I will provide what you need."

I have come across several other missionaries who were called with an audible voice and a great many others whose call was very definite and dramatic. I strongly believe every Christian worker needs to be called by the Lord. Many missionaries have left the field when things got tough because they were not certain they were in the right place. (This is especially true here in Colombia where most missionaries have left the field. We will not leave Colombia until God directs us to do so, not because the circumstances are dangerous or difficult.)

Our son Russell was growing up very precocious in every way. Before he was two, he could speak fluently, and I realized he was soon going to ask where God is. I told Patty when I went to work, "When Russell asks where God is, don't just tell him he's in heaven." Sure enough, that day Russell asked Patty, "Where does God live?"

Patty answered, "God lives in heaven, but He also lives in people's hearts.

Immediately Russell began to question, "Does he live in your heart?" Patty assured him that this was the case. Then Russell began questioning about our friends, until he finally asked about a little boy who was younger than he was. "I don't know if Jesus lives in Terry's heart, because I don't know if he has asked him yet," Patty replied.

With a very serious face, Russell asked the next question, "Does He live in my heart?"

"I don't think you have asked Him yet," was Patty's reply.

Immediately Russell dropped to his knees and prayed with a loud voice, "Come into my heart, Jesus! Come into my heart, God!" Then he got up and proclaimed with conviction, "He's in there!" This was the beginning of a remarkable and very fruitful Christian life.

Chapter II

The Miraculous Enters Our Lives

In our evangelical church with just over a hundred members, there were several men, including myself, who were very interested that the church would experience a revival. About six or eight men met early on Saturday morning to pray for revival. Russell, who was under five at this time, would not be left out and came and prayed the whole time on his knees.

God sent the revival, but not in the form we expected. We expected that either the pastor would catch fire or that some evangelist would come along and call the church to repentance. Instead, God sent a revival through the young people. Our young people's group numbered between 15 and 20. The church had to pump money into the young people's group continuously so they could have fun — Christian parties, outings, and occasionally a formal dinner to compete with the local high school prom. We brought in and paid for Christian music groups and rented buses to Christian activities, and generally subsidized the young people's group, arguing that this was better than losing them to the world.

The young people met on Sunday evening at 6:00 and then came up from the basement to join the evening service at 7:00. On this given Sunday, the young people came upstairs tremendously excited. The pastor decided to ask if anyone had a testimony. Usually getting anyone to testify in that church was like pulling teeth. The testimonies were separated by long, embarrassing silences. However this night almost all the young people were on their feet praising God. One young teenaged girl claimed she never really knew the Lord before that night. Everyone had assumed that she was a pillar of the young people's group. The pastor had to cut his message short to make room for all the young people who wanted to testify. After the meeting they didn't want to go home and gathered around the piano to sing and praise the Lord. They finally separated, agreeing to meet at the high school for prayer in the morning and to carry their Bibles to all of their classes.

What had happened was that the young peoples' group had experienced their own day of Pentecost. This was a dispensational church that believed that all miracles and gifts of the Spirit died out when the Scriptures were given. The young people realized that if the pastor and elders knew what had occurred among the young people, it would split the church, so they kept it quiet for over six months. The change in the young people was very dramatic. They were full of joy and praise to the Lord. They raised their own money with car washes and various other means. They even bought an old bus and repaired it for their outings, and on Sunday they drove it around and rounded up children for Sunday school. They challenged the adults to walk closer to the Lord. "Are you praising the Lord today, Brother Stendal," one young man asked me.

I replied honestly, "No, should I be?"

His response was, "Yes, because Psalm 34:1 says, '*I will bless the Lord at all times; His praise shall continually be in my mouth.*'"

As a Sunday school teacher, I was annoyed as they

began challenging the dispensational teachings of the church. "The miracles and gifts of the Spirit died out in the first century," I told them. One young man was adamant that this wasn't so. I expected the young people to just take my word for it as I was a church leader and well versed in dispensational teaching. We called the present dispensation, 'the silence of God.'

As the young man was not going to give in, in exasperation I pressed him as to how he knew the gifts were still operative today. His answer absolutely floored me. "Because I, myself, have spoken in tongues for up to 30 minutes at a time."

"Don't tell this to anyone," I cautioned, "It will split the church." It should be remembered that this took place in the fifties when anyone speaking of the gifts of the Spirit was considered to be of the devil by most churches.

The example of the dramatic change in the young people caused me to rethink my attitude on the dispensational teaching. I decided to go down to the Christian bookstore and check out what great Bible commentators had to say about the gifts of the Spirit. My favorite Bible commentator was G. Campbell Morgan. I started to read his commentary on I Corinthians 12. He said he didn't see any Biblical reason why the gifts shouldn't be operating today. My heart was greatly warmed and filled with joy as God showed me He was the same yesterday, today, and forever. A whole new world of faith opened before me, as I realized that God could do anything today that He had done in Biblical times. The lack of miracles today is due to lack of faith and holiness and hearing the Lord's voice, not due to reluctance on God's part. I have served the Lord in Colombia for 38 years and have seen hundreds of answers to prayer and miracles. For instance, when I am present in the Kogi tribe, I have prayed for and treated many Indians every day. I don't even know the funeral procedures of the Kogis, since I was never at a funeral.

If you believe that the age of miracles is over, then it is over for you because it depends on faith. By the way, any supposed faith healer who takes in large amounts of money and lives luxuriously is suspect. *He who says he abides in Him ought himself also to walk just as He walked.* I John 2:6 Let him come to some poor section of the world and exercise his supposed gift of healing freely among the poor and needy as the Lord did.

Eventually the pastor and elders found out that the young people were practicing the gifts of the Spirit, and sure enough, they threw them out, together with any adults that sympathized with them. I was not involved in this since I was up in Grand Rapids having my own problems previously mentioned at that time. This church in Bloomington had never sent out a missionary from their midst, but they threw out a number of young people who went on to become very fine missionaries. One in particular started a Bible Institute and founded many churches in Brazil.

Most of the people that were thrown out joined a very wonderful church called Bethany Missionary Church. This was a part of Bethany Fellowship that had a very interesting beginning. Five families were meeting in a basement and had an encounter with the Lord in which the Lord commissioned them to send out 100 missionaries. They founded a church with a missionary emphasis together with holiness and sanctification teaching. God will greatly bless any church that stresses holiness and evangelism.

This little church with five families tried to get together the funds to send out the first missionary, but they just couldn't set aside enough funds. They became frustrated and beseeched God in prayer to show them what they needed to do. The Lord showed them that they were putting their money in a pocket full of holes. He led them to consider living in community. In Minneapolis are some old mansions with four or five floors that wealthy families lived in at the turn of the century. Rich people no longer wanted these old houses, and they were too big for a normal family. Bethany bought one of these houses. They had everything in common. The husbands continued with their regular jobs, and the wives divided up the cooking and housekeeping responsibilities. Now there was only one yard to mow, one sidewalk to shovel, one real estate tax to pay, one telephone bill, etc. etc. Soon they were able to send out their first missionary.

Later they decided to buy a farm out beyond the city limits along the Minnesota River still maintaining their communal living. They decided to start a missionary training center. They wrote to missionary leaders all over the world and asked what training a missionary candidate should receive. The general consensus of replies stated that new missionaries arrived on the field with adequate Bible knowledge, but that they didn't know how to do practical things, work with their hands and repair and maintain things. This led Bethany to set up a training center where students studied half days and worked half days on the many commercial enterprises in which Bethany became involved. They made everything from electrical appliances to camping trailers. They wholesaled and distributed many products and founded an important publishing house.

Finally we finished the Farmington NIKE missile base, and I was assigned to the construction of the St. Anthony Falls high lift lock and dam right in the heart of Minneapolis. I was acting Project Engineer and then Office Engineer for this four year multimillion dollar project. We raised boats and barges 49 feet over the St. Anthony Falls. This was one of the highest lift locks in the world. The Gathun locks of the Panama Canal are only 24 feet high for comparison. Later on this project would be declared the best-constructed and most complex project in the nation. I loved the work I was doing.

I was receiving a fine salary, and I acknowledged that everything I had belonged to the Lord. I gave ten percent to my local church. I also set aside another ten percent to help missionaries or anyone in need. In order to do this, I had to downsize my living standards. The Lord helped us find a beautiful small gable end house with an attic room for the boys. This property also contained fruit trees, a garden plot, and many of the neighbors were Christians. I paid $650. down with a G.I. 4 ½ percent loan. It was close to our local church, and we were very happy there. I drove an old car that was a real trial in wintertime, but I was never late to work.

One evening I decided to teach Russell about missions. I had a book with large pages called *The Awakening Valley*. A reporter had recorded in pictures a week in the life of a Quechua Indian family. Their little one room mud hut was devoid of any possessions except for a cooking pot. Their little farm was quite dry and barren. On Sunday, market day, the man carried a long pole with a chicken tied on one end and some cooking bananas on the other. They hoped to sell this produce from their farm and get a little money to buy cooking oil and salt. They were able to market their goods, but the man got into a *cantina* with the money and started drinking it all up. Then he got into a machete fight and passed out on the way back to the farm for another week of the same.

Russell was just 4 ½ years old and had never seen anything like the things showed in the pictures. He was shocked and said, "Why do they live like that?"

"I don't know, Russell," I said, "I guess they don't know any better."

"Why don't they know any better?" was the next question.

"Well, Russell, I guess no one has ever brought them the Gospel."

He was shocked. "Why hasn't anyone brought them the Gospel?"

I was hard pressed for an answer. Finally, I said, "I guess nobody really cares for those Indians."

Now Russell was really shocked. "You care, don't you, Dad?"

I replied unconvincingly, "Yes, Russell, ... I ... care."

"Then why don't we go?" He meant like, right away. If there were people that bad off, and we could help them, then why didn't we help them? He had me pinned to the wall.

To get off the hook, I started making excuses. "You can't just go off to the mission field. There are things you don't understand, like visas, and finances, and God has to call you to be a missionary." I put a big emphasis on being called.

Russell realized that if the main thing holding up our helping poor Indian people was a call, he could fix that up right now. He got right down on his knees by the side of the couch and prayed in a loud voice. "Dear Lord, please call my parents to be missionaries."

God answered his prayer because he was praying in accord with the Biblical will of God. *Pray the Lord of the harvest to send out laborers into His harvest.* Matt. 9:38 Also, he was praying with childlike faith.

As I realized that God was calling us to the mission field, I shared this vision with Patty who was less than thrilled. "If you think that I'm going to the jungle with these three small children, you better think again. I can't even make it here with a washer and dryer. How could I handle primitive living conditions?" Russell who was not yet five years old, was the eldest of three children. In those days not everyone had an automatic washer and dryer. As the Lord was drawing me to a closer walk with Him, He showed me that to serve Him better, I should get rid of all unnecessary possessions. I sold my over and under shotgun and my .270 rifle and gave my .357 magnum pistol to a jungle missionary. With this money we bought the washer and dryer that Patty was so pleased with.

I was fascinated with the missionary stories of Sophie Mueller who worked with a number of tribes in the jungles of Colombia. I felt the Lord would have us work in Colombia where there were very few missionaries. Little did I realize that someday I would work with Sophie Mueller, as she turned over two of the tribes she was working with to me because they were too far away from the center of her work near the Brazilian border.

I didn't push things too hard with Patty but prayed that God would give her her own call to the mission field.

At this point Patty was having trouble with her hearing. However, she couldn't have a hearing aid because that would amplify the whole hearing range, and her hearing loss was only in the bass register. The bass register is where my voice range is. Patty had tuned me out. As I began inquiring about missions, Patty became more and more agitated. Finally she went to a doctor. He realized she was upset and asked her if there was anything bothering her. She told him, "My husband has this wild idea of going to the mission field."

The doctor was very understanding. He said, "In October, I am leaving for the Orient as a missionary doctor. My wife has gone through some of the same struggles that you are having. Your problem is that you think you are being called upon to do something you are not capable physically of doing. If it were a question of being short missionary support, you would have to pray it in or not go. You are going to have to ask the Lord to give you the strength necessary, or the Lord will have to change your husband's calling."

Patty joined a women's prayer group. They ran the group like an old time Methodist class meeting. There were some fine godly women in the group. Each member had to be honest about their spiritual condition. The first question was: Do you know the Lord? Patty could answer yes to that, but the next was more difficult. Do you have a pure heart?

Patty had just had a big argument with me and had

to admit she didn't have a pure heart. There were many attitudes and problems that Patty needed to confess and get the victory over. All this took a number of weeks. Patty described her heart as a basket of dirty laundry. As she picked up the top piece and repented of it and placed it on the cross of Calvary, she uncovered more dirty laundry underneath. It took a long time with all the women praying for her before she could say she had a pure heart. The women also told her that she needed to be subject to her husband. The last question was: Are you walking in victory? Finally, after working through all this with the help of the ladies in the prayer group, God gave Patty her own call to the mission field.

Chapter III

A Great Shake~Up

Walking in the Spirit in COLOMBIA

We were told by a Wycliffe Bible Translator who visited us, that Wycliffe had a linguistic school at the University of North Dakota during the summer. We began to make plans to attend. I would have to get a leave of absence from work. Just as we were about to apply, Patty said, "I want the Lord to send us the $15.00 registration fee that has to accompany each application from an unusual source as an assurance that God will take care of us if you quit your job." Women are always worried about security, and I couldn't talk her out of this 'fleece.' A few days later Patty found out that we had $15.00 more in our checking account than her records showed. "Do you think this is the unusual source?" Patty asked.

"It certainly is," I replied. All the other times she made errors in the checkbook, it resulted in our having less money than we thought. We decided to send my application to Wycliffe. There was a place to check if your wife would also be attending the course, and we trusted that they would understand that Patty was coming. As I took Russell to school that morning, he noticed the envelope to Wycliffe. He asked about it, and I told him it contained my application to the linguistic course. He immediately asked about his mother's application, and I told him that we didn't have the other $15.00 to send in her application yet.

"I want to take out $15.00 from my savings account and pay Mother's registration fee," he declared.

I called Patty from work and told her what had happened. "How can we take Russell's money?" I asked her.

She replied, "This morning, the Lord showed me why our wedding reception went so badly. I had some money in a savings account, and the Lord strongly impressed on me that I should give some or all of this money to Bob Pierce to send to buy Bibles for China just before Communism took over. I didn't do so because I thought my parents, who had given me the money, would be offended. Just before you called, I decided that if our children ever wanted to give from their small savings accounts, they should be allowed to do so."

The money that was in her savings account was what we used to pay for our wedding reception, which was a complete disaster. The cateress had several receptions scheduled for the same evening in June. The orders got mixed up, and we received two inexperienced girls with the wrong cake and no plates and silverware. Worst of all, they forgot to take the ice cream balls out of the dry ice and served them to the guests hard as a rock. Soon there were many pastel ice cream balls rolling on the floor.

The linguistic school at the University of North Dakota was extremely difficult, especially with three small children. Russell was very helpful taking care of the other children. One day I sent him to help Chaddy take a shower. Later I met him in the hall with a box of crackers. "I can't get Chaddy to take his clothes off, and I thought maybe the offer of some crackers would help," he explained.

When we sent Russell to a Christian school, we admonished him to do well because we had paid good money to send him there. Now the tables were turned, and Russell demanded that his mother get good grades because he had paid good money to get her there.

I told the Wycliffe directors that I was trained as a short field pilot and also was a civil engineer. The director said, "Pilots and construction men we can get, but if you can complete the linguistic work, our bottleneck is Bible translators." To my surprise, he said engineers made excellent Bible translators. Soon Patty and I completed the course and were on our way to Jungle Camp in southern Mexico. We had to build a house (*champa*) in the jungle with just vines and poles and thatch, but no nails. We learned how to handle dugout canoes and built rafts to float downriver. In a survival hike, we had to live off the land. Chaddy and Russell had a ball, and even Patty adapted well to the primitive conditions.

We felt called to Colombia and also felt led to join the Wycliffe Bible Translators. The only problem was that Wycliffe was not working in Colombia. We asked the Lord to clarify the problem to give us the assurance that we were being led by the Lord. An hour and a half after asking God's direction over this problem, the Wycliffe magazine which came out quarterly arrived with a headline — Newsflash: The Colombian government has just signed a contract with the Wycliffe Bible Translators to do linguistic work and Bible translation in all their tribes. This was a true miracle. Colombia had been closed to almost all evangelical mission work for its entire history.

We joined the Wycliffe Bible Translators and were some of the first missionaries assigned to Colombia. Wycliffe sent a letter to my local church asking them to help us raise the support we would need. The pastor never invited me to present our mission candidacy to the congregation nor acknowledged our call in any way. We had worked ten years in that church – teaching Sunday school, working with the Boys' Brigade and Pioneer Girls, youth sponsorers, children's church, president of the men's club, chairman of the missions' board, and generally doing everything we could. Patty wanted to change churches. When we went to study linguistics, we resigned from all work in the church except the 10th grade Sunday school class to which I felt a special attachment. I prayed, "Lord, if you want me to leave send someone to take over the 10th grade Sunday school class.

The next Sunday as new quarterlies were being distributed, a friend of mine said, "There are no new quarterlies for you. You are being relieved of your class. I had agreed with a friend that after Sunday school that day, I would go over to Bethany Fellowship and hear a famous holiness preacher from England. I felt betrayed and hurt. The message at Bethany was about resentment, and the only one at the altar was me. I called up the new teacher of the 10th grade class who was a friend of mine. She said she had never felt so led of the Lord as when she agreed to take the 10th grade class.

The Lord took me out of the church I was in, answered my prayer about the 10th grade class, and I found myself in Bethany. Here were the young people and adults who had been thrown out of the church while I was up north on a construction job. They welcomed me with open arms. We joined Bethany. We never dreamed they would help us get to Colombia. After all, they had 74 missionaries on the field, and we had not attended their Missionary Training Course. What we hoped to obtain from Bethany was prayer support.

I prayed about it, and the Lord showed me we should leave for Colombia in early January 1964. I made plane reservations to fly from Miami to Bogota, Colombia on January 3, 1964. We had only five dollars a month pledged at that time. (It never came in.) I took out my retirement fund from work (about $4,000.00) and invested it with some former missionaries to Peru who were ranching in North Dakota. They thought we could raise about half of our support with this investment in cattle, but it would take awhile to start paying off.

As I had returned back to my engineering job on the lock and dam after my leave of absence, I found a job offer in my in-basket. It was for the position of Chief Engineer for the Navy for all South Seas construction and was based on Guam. Guam was where I had spent time as a young lieutenant in the Corps of Engineers at the end of WWII. I met all the job description requirements, and I got all excited about the job. I called the procurement officer in charge of filling the job in San Francisco. When he found out what my job qualifications were, he got all enthusiastic. He said, "We've been trying to fill this job for six months. Just get a form 57 (job application) in to me, and the job is yours. It involved a large raise in pay plus extra overseas duty pay, and they would fly my family and me to Guam.

I discussed the matter with Patty and the family at supper. Russell immediately replied, "I thought God called us to be missionaries."

I said, "Russell, I can make enough money here to support several missionaries. The island is beautiful with white sand beaches and a wonderful climate and we can do Christian work in our spare time."

Russell replied, "Do we have to take the easy way?"

This rebuke from the mouth of little Russell caused me to rethink the job offer. However I kept the offer with its bright red attention getting border in my desk, and every once in awhile I would read it through again. Finally I decided to send in the application. Right then, Patty came down with pneumonia. Remembering back to the last time I disobeyed the Lord, and the result was pneumonia, I said, "O.K. Lord, we'll go to Colombia as Your missionaries. Immediately, Patty got well. Later, I found out that right after I would have gotten to Guam, a large typhoon hit Guam. I would have been in charge of the messy cleanup. Patty and the children would have been evacuated, and the extra money would have been dissipated maintaining two households.

One night after the evening service at Bethany, I was showing Russell the world map that Bethany had in the foyer. It was pretty impressive with 74 lights on it. Pastor Hegre came up behind me. He put his hand on my shoulder and said, "Well, we'll have to put a light up for Colombia pretty soon." I could hardly believe my ears. "How much support do you have?"

I was embarrassed to tell him $5.00 a month, so I said, "Very little."

He replied, "Well, you can count on us for $120. per month. In 1963 this was about half of what we needed. Bethany not only commissioned me and my whole family to the mission field, but they went right ahead and ordained me to the ministry. They told me the Lord showed them I would need this ordination. Patty and I were missionaries number 75 and 76 sent out by Bethany.

We went to the Colombian Embassy in Rochester, Minnesota. The consul was very friendly. He gave us a five-year visa instead of one year like everyone else had. When he found out we were going to study Spanish at the University of the Andes, he said, "The rector there is a very good friend of mine. He gave me his card on the back of which was a note to the rector saying, "Do everything you possibly can for this man.

In order to buy our tickets and meet our other expenses, I would have to collect a debt of $168.00 that an important businessman owed me in Farmington, and sell our car in Miami. The businessman didn't want to pay me. "You've got to pay me," I told him. "You owe it to me, and I can't get to Miami without it." Finally he snarled to his secretary to write me a check for $168.00. In Miami I found a returning missionary and sold our car for $300.00. Soon we were flying in a four-engine airplane over Colombia. It was daybreak, and I woke Russell up and showed him Colombia out the window. His reaction was, "We're really having fun now, aren't we, Dad?"

Chapter

IV

Needs Are Supplied

Walking in the Spirit in
COLOMBIA

The Spanish course at the University of the Andes was much more expensive than I had anticipated. I remembered the card of the Colombian consul. When the rector found out I was a civil engineer, he gave me a job teaching engineering in exchange for Patty's and my tuition in the Spanish course.

Soon I was put in charge of the construction of the new Wycliffe Translation Center called Lomalinda. We tied our hammocks between palm trees and went to work in April of 1964. I can't describe to you the feeling as I put a borrowed transit over my shoulder and began laying out a new project; this time for the Lord. I thought I had left engineering behind forever.

Lomalinda with its rolling hills and beautiful lake, surrounded by jungle, was a tropical paradise, especially for young boys like Chaddy and Russell. Just the variety of pets they could have here was awesome. In addition to parrots and monkeys, there were toucans, and land boa constrictors with their beautiful orange and black markings. The marmoset, which was the size of a chipmunk, slept all day in Gloria's pocket to the amusement of her friends at school. Chaddy had an alligator pond with an island in the middle. When Pastor Art Sather asked Chaddy in front of the whole church in Everett, Washington, "Chaddy, what good are all those alligators?" Chaddy, who was 11 years old responded, "They work to trim the hedge."

Chaddy's pet cotamundi slept in his bed, and

wouldn't let anyone come near it. I had the best Indian hunters train Chaddy and Russell in jungle hunting which is usually done over bait at night. Some of the other translators were shocked, but no missionary can equal the rapport the boys have with Indians, as well as local Colombian people. This probably explains how we are now able to work and operate FM and AM radio stations in the middle of an area noted for violence. The boys also learned mechanics and farming and many other things from the skilled workers that came from the States to do the day-to-day work, so that the translators could devote full time to translation.

I found out from the missionary nurse that attended Patty when Gloria was born that there was an isolated tribe of Indians living in the Sierra Nevada de Santa Marta. This whole story of how God opened the door to this resistant Kogi tribe, complete with a very special airstrip is written in *High Adventure in Colombia*, and is available from Ransom Press, International. (See back of book.)

After five years of walking in the Spirit in Colombia, I felt led to return to the United States and complete a master's degree in linguistics with a minor in anthropology. To complete the thesis on the Kogi language, I would need my language helper, Alfonso, to accompany me to the States. Patty said, "You can't go back to the University of North Dakota, you don't have any money." I replied in faith, "They don't even ask for the tuition for ten days."

Our Wycliffe office was very negative about our taking Alfonso to the States. They said it would take two months to get the paper work done. We needed a passport and a visa, and we didn't even have a birth certificate. I found a lawyer on the north coast who said he could get a birth certificate. He had both Patty and me sign a long fine print document. When I finally got around to reading the document, I discovered that we had signed an affidavit stating that we had been present at Alfonso's birth!

The next step was the passport. As Alfonso and I waited in a long line, the head of the passport division saw me in the line and stopped to ask what an American was doing in a Colombian passport line. I told him Alfonso needed a passport to go with me to the States. He told me what papers we would need and told us to come back the next morning with the papers, and he would issue the passport in the afternoon. I later found out it normally took weeks to issue a passport. The Lord helped us with the U.S. visa as well. In two days, Alfonso was ready to travel with us to the States.

Traveling in an old car, we arrived at the graduate school of the University of North Dakota. A friend of mine was in charge of supplying speakers for local churches. He gave me the best ones, and I had the tuition by the time I needed to pay it. One Sunday I preached in three churches and a camp meeting. One Sunday we went to a little church on the edge of town. David Riveness, the pastor, met us on the steps and took one look at my family and Alfonso and said, "Are you folks missionaries?" I had on a suit and tie that I had worn before I went to Colombia, totally out of date. "Could you come to the evening service and tell us about your work?" Dave added.

Dave had a struggle that night because he had brought a new organ to the church that morning, and he hoped to use the evening offering towards the down payment on the organ. However the Holy Spirit was telling him to give the offering to the poor missionary family that showed up on his doorstep. Finally he gave the offering to us. The next day a businessman in the congregation called Dave and asked, "How much did that organ cost that you had in the morning service?" Dave told him, and the man responded, "I liked that organ; it added a lot to the service. You'll have a check for that amount in the mail."

Dave was the director of the summer camp that his church conference sponsored. He had tried six different friends to get a speaker for the camp with no success. Finally he called his old friend, Art Sather, who agreed to come. The Monday morning after I spoke in the church, Art called Dave. He said, "I want you to go to the University of North Dakota and locate a man named Chad Stendal who is attending there."

"That won't be too hard," Dave responded. "He spoke in our church last night." The church had agreed to send Alfonso and our children to camp, and so Dave said, "Furthermore Art, one of those Kogi Indians you have been praying for so long will be under your ministry at camp." Art and his wife, Verdie, had received a message from the Lord through tongues and interpretation that the Word of God should be sent to a little people living high in the mountains with strange customs. They had been praying for the Kogis ever since.

Soon Art was in Grand Forks, and he was fascinated to see slides of the Kogis and to meet Alfonso. Art and I hit it off, and he said, "We have to share all this at the closing meeting of the camp. There will be about 250 people there. I'll tell my part of God calling us to prayer for this tribe, then you introduce Alfonso (who was in his tribal clothes) and tell how God opened the door to this tribe."

I said, "I have agreed to speak to two Presbyterian

churches next Sunday, and we need to get a map and see if I can be at the camp by 2:00 p.m. Sure enough, God had worked everything out, and there would be just enough time after the second church service to get to the camp. The audience at the camp sat transfixed as Art preached for an hour. I followed with another hour, and soon everyone was praising the Lord for His miraculous dealings with the Kogi tribe. I still had time to get back to Grand Forks in the evening to speak at the Baptist church.

Art invited Alfonso and me to his church in the Seattle area. There followed a remarkable series of meetings in many churches. In the Philadelphia Church, Pastor Roy Johnson turned over the Sunday morning service to us, which he had never been known to do before for a missionary. We not only had the church full, but also the aisles and dozens of young people turned their lives over to the Lord for full time service.

During our first two terms on the mission field, God supplied all our need, sometimes to the penny. We decided to make our needs known only to God in prayer and not mention money unless somebody asked. As we contemplated returning to Colombia for our second term, we were short about $200 dollars per month. We prayed about it, and soon Art Sather asked about our finances. He said, "How much do you need?" I said that if we really watched our expenditures, we could get by with another $200.dollars a month. "We'll pick it up." He said. We lived very simply in the tribe, taking advantage of locally grown food such as platano, yuca, malanga, and arracacha. Some of the food is completely unknown in the States and took some getting used to before you could eat it. Wild game also supplemented our diet. One familiar item of food, readily available among the Kogis was the banana. Since they preferred to boil them while they were green, as soon as they started to turn yellow, they brought them to us. We always had more bananas than we could eat. I insisted that none be wasted, so Patty and the kids had to eat many bananas a day. Some of the children still can't stand bananas. Later on, Patty became adept at making 'banana bread' using mostly local ingredients, and incorporating as many ripe bananas as possible. All the visiting Kogis loved this delicacy, and I am told that some are still making 'banana bread' today, using homemade ovens.

Chapter V

We Become Airborne

Walking in the Spirit in COLOMBIA

During our second term on the field, my Master's degree arrived, and the director decided to make me Tribal and Technical Studies Coordinator in charge of all tribal work and technical studies. As I visited the various tribal sites, I often found one of two extremes. Sometimes the team devoted too much attention to linguistic work, and not enough attention to the needs of the Indians. I sometimes had to reprimand, "If you are not going to be living examples of the Scriptures you have come to translate, you should go home." Occasionally the opposite attitude would prevail. There would be such close identification with the people, even lack of sanitation and such primitive basic living conditions that the linguistic work would be impeded.

After the work day at Lomalinda was over at 5:00 p.m., most everybody played volleyball. I decided it would be a lot more useful to visit our Colombian neighbors. I found an old Paez Indian who was a pastor in his tribe, and together with Alfonso and my family we proceeded along the trail (Indian file of course) the ¾ mile to the nearest house. We held meetings for 30 consecutive nights with nobody receiving the Lord. As a Wycliffe member, I wasn't supposed to preach, but I could pray and encourage everyone. The 30th night, we found the woman of the house deathly sick. I diagnosed it as pneumonia. With great difficulty, I was able to talk the director into allowing the nurse to let me have a penicillin shot to treat her. We prayed for her and injected her, and the next night she was perfectly well, and her 17 year-old son became our first convert.

Soon dozens of people were receiving the Lord, and people were going from house to house evangelizing. We were into what is called a 'people's movement.' We appointed elders and deacons, and things were going very well until we started to get opposition from several sources. First, one of the largest missions in Colombia had a small church in the area. The Colombian superintendent demanded that all the new converts attend his local church. We had not told any of the converts where they should attend church, but we made it clear that anyone wishing to attend a local church was free to do so. Not too many wanted to attend this church. The Colombian superintendent became very angry with me and said he was going to Bogota to get my visa cancelled and see to it I was kicked out of the country. This time when I was attacked, I could rejoice in accordance with Matthew 5:12 *Rejoice and be exceeding glad, for great is your reward in heaven. . .* Something I was unable to do in Grand Rapids. I now realized that these attacks came because I was walking close enough to the Lord to be a threat to Satan. Nothing came of the threat to have me expelled from the county.

Then the Wycliffe director got notice of the revival and called me in. "Stendal, we are supposed to be working with Indians, not Spanish-speaking Colombians. The whole area around our translation center is full of believers. Did you have anything to do with this?" I tried to assure him that the Lord had done it, and I had not preached in Spanish or done anything against Wycliffe principles. The director was worried that Wycliffe would be kicked out of the country. I told him God would respond for the believers that He had brought to Himself. Indeed, Wycliffe was accused of a great number of things over the years, but never of being Christian proselytizers. The rumors were rampant as to what this base was there for. The press accused it of being a CIA base. Since Wycliffe was not engaged in obvious Christian activities, what were they doing with 77 buildings and over 300 people, including children? Were they a missile base? Had they discovered uranium on the bottom of the lake, or what? One day navy helicopters arrived and out came navy frogmen with submachine guns. They made a grid of the lakebed and the frogmen examined the whole lake, and of course they found nothing. The Wycliffe method was to concentrate on the translation process, relying on other missions to utilize the translation and establish churches. As I inspected various tribal sites, it became clear to me that because Colombia had been closed to missions for so long, for the most part there were not any other missions to come along and utilize the translations.

I decided to resign from Wycliffe and concentrate on the distribution problem before the translations became unused and ended up in cartons in a warehouse. To obtain a new visa apart from Wycliffe sponsorship was considered an impossible task. All I could find was a window to submit the extreme amount of paperwork required, and there was nobody to give any help in filling out the forms. I prayed about it, and the Lord showed me how to proceed. I found an open stairway to the second floor from which you could look down into the cubicles of the immigration service. I tried to figure out who was in charge, and soon it became clear who was running things. I stood by the door to the immigration service where I knew this man would have to come out sooner or later. As he stepped out the door,

I asked him, "Can you recommend someone who can help me with the paper work to obtain a visa?" He said his roommate did this work, and soon I had a resident visa as a rancher and linguist. I didn't even have to leave the country and apply from outside which is normally required.

The Wycliffe director didn't really want us to leave. Patty had a dream of the director giving us his blessing to leave, and shortly after this, that is just what he did.

We obtained a beautiful homestead for $4,000 dollars, and my plan was to give 10 acre plots to each Christian worker and plant cacao to support them. Cacao is what chocolate comes from. I went to western Colombia and obtained disease resistant seeds. We planted each seed in a small plastic bag full of rich black soil. We put up the laths overhead to provide the necessary partial shade. The three-month dry season was upon us, and we left three national workers whose job it was to water the plants each day.

For eleven years, I had worked with Indians. I was not prepared for what would happen trying to work with rural Spanish speaking nationals. Even though watering the plants was all they had to do, they didn't do it, and the plants dried up and died. At this time we were trying to live in community with a number of Colombian families. We tried to practice the Sermon on the Mount and prefer the others before ourselves and take the lowest position. The families we had taken in stomped all over us. However we personally learned many lessons from the Lord, developing our own characters. Professing national Christians from various missions came to work with us. We accepted them as Christians. This was a mistake. Chaddy, our second son, was the most adapt at sizing up Colombians. He said,

"Dad, some of these professing Christians are phony and just waiting to rip you off with false claims for wages and benefits at the labor office. We learned hard lessons of how to get along with rural Colombians.

At this time we were having great success with the Guyabero and Guajibo tribes. Sophia Mueller, the famous missionary to the Indians, had turned over to us the care of about 600 Indians living in our area of the Guaviari River. She was very occupied with the Curipaco, Piunavi, and Cubeo tribes way to the east of Colombia. Sophie entered Colombia as a young woman. Somehow she obtained a visa and then the government denied visas to her coworkers. She hired a dugout canoe and floated down the Guaviari River until she came to the Curipaco Indians. Her only possessions were a change of clothes and a soup bowl and a spoon. When the Indians cooked up a meal, she brought her bowl, and they filled it up for her. She also carried powdered milk and vitamins. She was probably the most successful Indian worker of all time. She worked over 50 years in the jungle and died not too long ago. The example of Sophie as recorded in her mission magazine *Brown Gold* was an inspiration to me when I was an engineer. It was a dream come true to continue her work on the upper Guaviare.

Sophie had translated the New Testament into six different tribal languages. In some of them she had a 98% literacy rate and a 100% conversion rate. In her New Testaments she had interspersed questions to make sure the Indians didn't just read without understanding. She appointed elders. In addition to singing and prayer, the services had a unique way of studying the Scriptures. Sophie divided each village into four parts. These formed a square with teenagers, women, young men, and elders on the four sides. Then each side took turns reading the Scripture and asking the questions in the text to one of the other groups.

Perhaps the most interesting and colorful of Sophie's methods was the quarterly conference. It was the job of the host village to secure enough fish and wild game to feed the other local villagers for one week. As each village group arrived singing, marching single file with their elders carrying banners, the welcoming villagers ran out to meet them and lined up also in a single line, shaking hands with each one as they passed by, thus greeting each newcomer. It was a also a time of evangelism as new Indians showed up for the conference. All sorts of games and competitions, including blow guns and bow and arrows took place. At the end of the week we had a baptismal service followed by communion.

To speed up the work, we decided to ask the Lord for an airplane. We promised the Lord that if He would give us a plane, we would never deny passage to anyone in an emergency whether they could pay or not. We had just experienced a very exasperating experience with an airplane from a mission operating in our area. The pilot refused to fly out a friend of ours who was having a medical emergency because we didn't have the money on the spot out in the jungle. I said to the pilot, "I will get you the money as soon as I get back to town." He replied, "Sorry, Chad, but our mission policy is not to fly anyone without the money in hand."

The Lord helped us acquire a plane. We found out that a widow was selling her dead husband's airplane in Cali. I immediately flew over there, and the rich widow was very understanding when I explained our missionary work and agreed to sell us the plane for the very cheap price of $6,000 dollars. It was a 1952 Cessna 170 with less than 2,000 hours total time on it. The only problem was that I didn't have $6,000 dollars. I asked if she would hold it for me for three weeks while I raised the money. I returned to the States, and a number of churches helped us out. One pastor said, "Our missionary pilot in Liberia just sent a request for $6,000 dollars to replace the propeller on his plane, and you're going to obtain a whole airplane for $6,000 dollars?"

I got back to Cali with the $6,000 dollars two days before the deadline. Because the plane was already in Colombia, we saved all the time and expense of importing it. A mechanic at the Cali airport had said, "This plane would be worth a lot more money if it only had a current license. When I came to take possession of the plane, there was on the pilot's seat a new, just issued license. I couldn't believe it. The license had been pending and tied up with paper work for months, but there it was, right on the day I needed it. The civil aeronautics issued Russell and me Colombian pilot's licenses for six months, based on our U.S. licenses.

The plane was not very fast, and two cylinders were cracked, but we could fly anywhere in the jungle, just as expensive commercial and missionary aircraft could do. We flew that plane over some of the most hazardous jungle and mountain terrain for over seven years, and it never let us down. The chief pilot of a mission warned me, "Chad, flying is a full time job. Either be a pilot or a missionary, but don't try to do both. I've had several friends who tried to do both, and they all cracked up. We put close to 7,000 hours on several airplanes without cracking up. The average time between serious accidents for both missionary and civil aircraft in the Colombian jungle is about 1350 hours.

What was the secret of the remarkable safety the Lord has provided for our whole family, as well as the plane? We've had many close calls. We have never hesitated to put our lives or our material possessions at the service of others in need. To give you some idea of the dangerous situations we have been living under in the *llanos* (plains) of eastern Colombia, Chaddy told me that he counted up 23 friends he knew when we first came. They are all dead now except for three who left the area. None of the half dozen commercial pilots who were flying the area when we came are still alive.

When the guerrillas took over our area, they killed many who were not committed to their cause. They might have killed us, except that they decided to kidnap Russell, thinking that because we had an airplane, we must have money. They left Chaddy and me alone, because we were the ones that were supposed to raise a half million dollars for Russell's release. After several months the guerrillas had a secret meeting to decide whether or not to kill Russell because we didn't have any money, a lower ranking leader defended Russell and said, "You're not killing him. He's the one who flew my mother to the hospital when we didn't have any money." Russell had a lot of time to think and meditate while he was kidnapped. He asked the Lord, "Why didn't our plane go down during all this time?" The Lord showed him that because we had mercy on those in need, He had mercy on us. *Blessed are the merciful, for they shall obtain mercy.* Matt. 5:7 . After a few more weeks Russell was released and a top guerrilla commander told Chaddy, "We were mistaken about you. You and your brother are free to come and go as you please among us." For the past eighteen years this promise has been honored.

Chapter VI

'Crocodile Dundee'

Chaddy is the 'Crocodile Dundee' of the Colombian jungle. He grew up there and can equal or out do the Indians in all jungle activities. Chaddy has become a legend in all of eastern Colombia. Early in his life, he made conscious decisions to identify with the poor people. When he was eleven, I brought him to the nearest town to Lomalinda. On a very long wall encompassing the school was the following message scrawled on the wall: The Gringos ride around on motorcycles while our children go barefoot. From that date on, Chaddy took off his shoes to go barefoot and identify with the common people. He still does.

He is always ready to give a helping hand to whomever needs it. He is also very courageous and tough. While helping a neighbor inoculate his cattle, a mad cow charged Chaddy. He waited until the last minute, then stepped aside, and as the cow went by, he grabbed it by the tail and pulled it sideways off its feet. because of the cow's great speed, they both flew through the air and landed in a heap. When the dust cleared, one of Chaddy´s feet was twisted 180 degrees with the heel forward and the toes backward. He turned the leg around by hand and made cardboard splints to hold it in place while he rode his dirt bike cross-country to the hospital three hours away. X-rays showed four broken bones – one in his leg and three in his ankle. Once he drove to town with a bad toothache. Finding the local dentist too drunk to pull his tooth, he pulled it himself with a pliers, while looking in his jeep's rear view mirror.

One time while he was crossing a swamp at night on a log, his dog Trotsky had to pass through the stream, and a large anaconda wrapped around him. Chaddy went into the swamp without a flashlight and fought the anaconda, until it released his dog.

It is some kind of miracle that Chaddy has been allowed to continue working in a guerrilla-controlled area. When Russell was released from being kidnapped, Chaddy spoke to the guerrilla leadership, "If you want me to leave, I will leave, but I would really like to stay." The guerrilla commander replied, "You don't have to leave, Chaddy. You've never been a gringo (an arrogant American). It also helped that Chaddy is an excellent mechanic and can repair just about anything. It is due to Chaddy that we have been able to operate a radio station for three years in an area where the guerrillas could close us down at any time.

One time Chaddy broke some bones in his shoulder out at the farm, and it had healed somewhat leaving much of his arm numb. As Chaddy and his friend, Raul, were taking the bus back to Bogota to seek medical treatment, a big truck came downhill the other way. They met on a bridge that was too narrow for both of them. The bus went over the side into a total abyss of hundreds of feet straight down. I had a little joke about a preacher who slid off the side of a cliff into midair, "Lord save me, he cried!" The car smashed up on the rocks below, but the preacher was unharmed. As he looked at the totally destroyed car, he exclaimed in dismay, "I forgot to pray for the car."

The bus was in free fall, and then turned end for end four times. Chaddy remembers sliding from front to back of the bus four times, sliding on the ceiling of the bus. Chaddy remembered my story and prayed, "Lord save me and Raul!" as the bus went through the air. Then he got convicted that this was really a selfish prayer and added, "And don't let anyone be killed!"

Finally the bus stopped, suspended by a little tree, beyond which was a drop of hundreds of feet. It was dark, and gasoline fumes were everywhere. Chaddy shouted, "Don't anyone light a match!" Everyone was injured except Chaddy and Raul. One by one they got the passengers out of the bus. Then they had to carry them up a steep bank to the road. Chaddy used his good shoulder to lift some of the injured. After awhile the police arrived and commandeered cars to take the injured back to the hospital in Villavicencio.

The police asked Chaddy and Raul what they wanted to do. "We'd like to continue on to Bogota," they responded. The police stopped the next bus and said, "These men have already paid their fare to the bus that's over the side." Early in the morning, Chaddy arrived at Russell's apartment in Bogota where Russell had invited a doctor over for breakfast to have a look at Chaddy's shoulder. Russell was used to Chaddy looking a little disheveled coming in from the jungle, but this time took the cake. There was blood, dirt and bruises all over him.

Chaddy had a lot of work to do back in the *llanos*. He had Russell, the doctor and other believers pray for him, and he returned to the jungle, and his shoulder healed.

Chaddy Takes Me Fishing
The boys discovered a beautiful lake in the jungle.

They called it *Ariscos* or Wild Place. It was guarded at both ends by waterfalls. The lower end, leading to the Guaviari River had fast moving water and big boulders. Only Chaddy had been able to navigate through it with his outboard motor at full throttle, making rapid and dangerous turns until he entered a beautiful lake about a mile and a half across. The upper end came out of a high bluff in the jungle and had a series of smaller waterfalls, kind of like a huge water slide. Chaddy thought it might make a good tourist attraction. This was before the guerrillas had taken over. Chaddy decided to bring me there with my rod and reel and see if the lake was good for sport fishing. He cleared the brush off of a high bluff, and I landed the plane there.

Armando was in the front of the dugout canoe, and Chaddy was in the stern. The first cast I made had a hard strike, and I knew I had an unusually powerful fish on the line. After awhile it got away, and when I reeled in, the hooks on my lure had been straightened out. Next I decided to use a floating plug, called a bassarino, great for bass back in Minnesota. I had another hard strike, and when I reeled in, my plug had been bit in two.

I got out a big, strong spoon used for muskies back in Minnesota. I had another hard strike. This time it was a payara over yard and a half long. It would leap clean out of the water in spectacular jumps. This is the fish with huge front teeth several inches long that protrude out the top of his head. As I was fighting the gigantic fish, he worked himself to the edge of the jungle, and with a mighty leap of about 8-feet high, the lure caught in a branch of a tree higher than we were, and the fish fell free. Armando and Chaddy were beside themselves with laughter, "Look what that payara did with Dad's lure. He stuck it up in the tree for him."

The lake was very deep, and we decided to troll for big cachama, a big, round fish that could go over 50 pounds. Soon I had one on. He was so strong, I couldn't brake him. He ran all my line out with a zing, and soon all I had was a reel with no line.

We decided that to fish *Arriscos*, we would need especially strong mustad hooks filed to a sharp point to enter those tough mouths. We were not sure if American fishermen were ready for 'The Wild Place.' Maybe if we didn't mention the anacondas and jaguars, they would come.

This section of the *Guaviari* has the largest snakes in the world. We found out that a zoo was offering a thousand dollars a foot for any snake over 20 feet long. We captured a 22-foot anaconda, but it escaped from its pen into the adjacent pig pen. Soon it had a pig in its coils. One of Chaddy's workers wanted to save the pig and shot $22,000.00 in the head.

Chapter VII

We Have Wheels Also

Once we got a plane, Russell decided we should make ourselves self-sufficient. The river was full of fish that no one could get to market because the problems of transportation were too difficult. Russell decided that with a freezer at the river, we could fly frozen fish to market. He started studying refrigeration and soon designed a large walk-in freezer with the refrigerator and generator in perfect balance. This was a great benefit to the whole area. Christian Indians and the colonists of the area could all catch a fish and sell it to us if they needed a shirt or machete or whatever. We were able to meet all our flight expenses for many years through this fish business. In all that time, we never had a planeload of fish spoil or the freezer go down for repairs or lack of fuel. Once again the Lord supernaturally looked out for us. We kept a large group house in the town of San Martin. I had essentially traded houses when I left Wycliffe. I sold the house I had built in Lomalinda and purchased Wycliffe's very large house and warehouse in San Martin. This large house was always full of sick Indians and colonists from the jungle. The Lord enabled us to maintain this house and all our flying through the fish business. In San Martin we provided cheap protein through the fish to the poor people who had been priced out of the meat market. In fact, the local priest used to thank and praise us from the pulpit on Fridays and Easter!

Unknown to us, the guerrillas were infiltrating our area. They overran our fish house, and later kidnapped

Russell. It is interesting to note that when the guerrillas came to the fish house, it didn't have any fish in it because it was being cleaned. The Lord closed the door on that chapter of our lives without ever having the loss of fish through spoilage. The whole story of Russell's kidnapping is covered in the two books, *Rescue the Captors* by Russell, and *The Guerrillas Have Taken Our Son,* by Patty and me. *Rescue the Captors* was written by Russell while he was a captive of the guerrillas. The guerrillas became so interested in what Russell was writing that they would fight over the pages as Russell finished them on an old typewriter the guerrillas had obtained who knows where. Russell alternated chapters between what was happening with the kidnapping and our life in Colombia as missionaries to the Indians. This helped the guerrillas understand what we were doing and helped to get Russell released.

After Russell's kidnapping, David Riveness, who was now pastoring in Wetaskiwin, Alberta, Canada, called me up. "Chad, many people and churches have been praying for Russell's release. You just have to come up here and tell us all about it"

Russell, Marina, and Patty all agreed that they did not want to go to Canada. I said, "These people have been praying faithfully for us, and we have a moral obligation to go. Patty, always interested in practical matters said, "You don't even have transportation to get there." The next place we spoke was in Austin, Minnesota, and I mentioned that we needed a car. An Iowan farmer said that he had an old Buick he wasn't using. Soon we were off for the area of Edmonton, Alberta. There was so much interest in hearing about Russell's kidnapping that we had to split up. Russell and Marina went east as far as Moose Jaw, and Patty and I went northwest as far as Fort St. John.

This marked a new phase of our ministry. As a Bible translator, I had learned a lot that was valuable to other Christians. I began to receive requests to do Bible seminars on different books of the Bible. I would start on Sunday morning and end on Wednesday evening. I could usually interest the people sufficiently on Sunday that they would come back on Monday, Tuesday, and Wednesday evenings. Sometimes I would start in another church on Thursday evening and go Friday and Saturday evenings and finishing up on Sunday. Actually, I am still available for this kind of ministry.

Churches opened up to us as far away as the Inuit (Eskimos) in the Northwest Territories of Canada. I found that pastors of little rural churches needed fellowship, but they were afraid that anyone coming into the area was going to start a rival work and steal their sheep. Since my main work was in Colombia, they could relax. Also, distances were great and offerings modest, so not even music groups could make a go of it. By this time we had written four books. We could make our expenses through the sale of the books. Then the offerings could go to our mission work. Our financial situation had suffered with the loss of the fish business, but little by little a few churches and many individuals began helping with our support. The Lord laid us on the hearts of many people, which no doubt contributed to the success of our mission work. I want to stress that I didn't plan any of this, but looking back on it, the hand of the Lord is very evident.

In Colombia, one of our good Colombian friends, Ricardo Trillos, had an interesting idea. One of the most liked Hollywood films in Colombia was Walt Disney's "Love Bug." Ricardo thought that if we could get a white Volkswagen and fix it up to imitate the 'Love Bug,' we would have something that would attract crowds of young people, children, and adults for a presentation of the Gospel. With great difficulty, I got the funds together, and Chaddy and Russell worked on the tandem controls and hydraulic cylinders. Soon *Maliquias* (Malachi), as we called the car was ready. It was driven from the back seat using tandem controls. Tinted glass kept people from seeing the real driver and gave the impression that the car was being driven with no driver. Hydraulic cylinders opened and shut the doors. The car could bow down and rise up. It could tilt 30 degrees to either side. On top were flashing lights and a siren we had gotten off a police car. Of course a large P.A. system completed the equipment. We would drive the car around the town we wanted to evangelize, inviting people to the meeting in the town square, apparently with no driver. We would then arrive at the town square with lights flashing and the siren blazing because we were in a spiritual emergency. We always had between several hundred to a thousand people there. When the invitation was given, usually about 50% of the people made a commitment.

We also had invitations from the schools, police stations, and military barracks. The commanding general of the police, who was an evangelical and a friend of ours, sent an order to all police stations to fall out their agents and give a half hour or as much time as we needed to evangelize. The high schools, both public and private, were delighted to have us. We would start off in their main assembly room. What was said in the first few minutes was crucial to maintain the interest of high schoolers. Ricardo would start by saying, "Russell here is ready to tell you what it was like to be captured by the guerrillas and held for ransom." Then he would tell them that if they really didn't want to be there, they could leave for a designated study hall. A few would leave, but now the rest were there of their own free will. A room was set aside the next morning for those who wanted to know more about following the Lord.

In the afternoon Malachi would give a short demonstration of all it could do, followed by a short challenge with Malachi apparently preaching. Everyone was then told to invite their parents for an evening meeting. Often the high schools were large with disciplinary problems and gangs. Once the teachers and parents found out that they had less disciplinary problems after we had been there, we had more invitations to schools than we could handle.

The same was true of churches. We were invited to some of the largest cathedrals in the country. This started in Zipaquera, the home of the salt mines of Colombia. An earthquake had damaged the large intricate gold, ornamental altar. A priest who was expert in this kind of repairs came from Rome to fix the altar. He tried everything and finally knelt before the altar, asking the Lord as to what he should do. After some time meditating, the Lord showed him the altar wasn't important. Even the beautiful cathedral wasn't vital. It was the people that were important. This was a great insight, and the priest began to experience a personal awakening to the things of God.

Somehow the priest heard about Malachi and Russell and Ricardo and invited them to come and hold meetings. Ricardo, who is very impetuous, thought of a way to wake up this Catholic congregation. When Catholics say the Lord's Prayer, they usually mumble along, not thinking of the significance of the words. Ricardo took the big red flashing signal light off of Malachi. Then he had somebody turn off the lights

The Lord begins to call us to be Missionaries *1961*

The house we made out of jungle materials in Chiapas, Mexico.

1963

The first little house that Chad made in Lomalinda.

1965

A Matter of Life or Death

Our whole family
on the trail to
live with the Kogis.

1965

Mariana's family
who became
some of the
first Christians.

1971

Because of the
healings, they made
me a Kogi chief.

1971

*A Matter
of Life
or
Death*

Chad operated a used
Helio Courier for a few
months, but it was too
expensive. 1976

Hundreds of Guajibos
and Guayaberos
attended the
conference at Chaparral
(our farm). 1978

A village of Guayaberos
arrives At our farm for
the Christian conference,
marching behind
their banner. 1978

A Matter
of Life
or
Death

Chad, our daughter Gloria, and Roberto at the Caribbean Sea.

1978

Chaddy makes a dugout canoe in the jungle.

1981

We maintained our Cessna 182 with proceeds from our fish business.

1982

A Matter of Life or Death

Our daughter, Sharon, after receiving her R.N. degree, helped us in the Sierra.

1982

Chaddy finally found the girl of his dreams Yolanda.

1987

Our son-in-law, Bob, Alfonso, and Chad work on the Kogi New Testament.

1987

A Matter of Life or Death

Our A-frame house
and short airstrip in
Mamarongo

1988

Chad, Pat, and Russell
with two Eskimo friends
at the Arctic Ocean.

1989

Malachi, our talking car
drew large crowds for
evangelistic meetings.

1990

A Matter
of Life
or
Death

The church that Chad built in San Martin in the *llanos.* 1995

The day that Chaddy brought Ray Rising to our house, directly from the guerrillas. 1996

Russell and his family on one of the many ministry trips to the north. 1997

A Matter of Life or Death

Alfonso and his whole family, including three grandchildren.

2002

Four presentations of the Spanish Bible, and the Christian print shop that does all our literature.

2002

The FM radio tower on the hill and the AM antenna in the vall at the new Lomalinda. These are two of the four stations that broadcast 24 hours a day.

2002

A Matter of Life or Death

when the congregation droned on reciting the Lord's Prayer. Right when everyone came to the part 'forgive us our trespasses, as we forgive those who trespass against us.' Ricardo turned on the bright flashing red light from the car. He told the startled congregation that there was a red light on the play, a stoplight and a condition in the Lord's Prayer. If they expected God's forgiveness, they had to forgive everyone that had done anything to them. The Spirit of the Lord came down, and soon people were contacting old enemies to forgive them. They brought Malachi right into the huge cathedral, and people were flocking to the meetings.

They decided to have a night for men only, and the church filled up with men. On this particular night, the bishop attended to see what these evangelicals were doing in one of the churches of his diocese. When the old bishop saw the church full of men praising the Lord, he said it was the greatest miracle he had seen in his priesthood. Usually Catholic churches have mostly women and children attending. He said, "If this is what you are doing, all the other cathedrals and churches are open to you." And so began an incredible ministry in dozens and dozens of churches. Ricardo is still carrying on this ministry, but Russell is deeply engaged in a ministry involving literature and radio transmission.

The Malachi ministry went on for over seven years. I remember one two-year period when we conducted 50 campaigns of usually a week each year. We estimate Malachi reached about 350,000 people. These were not people bussed in to some rally, but ordinary people right off the streets of most of the towns of Colombia. People just loved Malachi. Malachi was awesome at night with an interior blue light iluminating the empty driver's seat, and all the other red and blue flashing lights. We had to install a sprinkler system to get people to step back so we could drive out. We had the Ten Commandments on the hood of the car. A number of priests were converted, especially when they realized the Ten Commandments had been changed, and the part about no graven image had been removed from the catechism. Several priests took down their statues of saints, and one even bricked up the niches they had been in. In one church, the people tried to kill the priest who had to barricade himself in the church.

Of all the hundreds of meetings, certain special times stand out. One of these was the time Malachi visited the emerald mines. Russell was invited to visit the emerald mines together with the local governor to find a place to build a hospital. Russell had access to equipment to set up hospitals left over from the cold war. After a sumptuous banquet, the mine owner invited the guests to visit the open face of the area where emeralds were being mined. It was traditional to allow guests to take an emerald from the working face, if they could find one. Russell was very short of funds at that time and thought if he could find an emerald, it would help his finances. However he felt from the Lord an urgency to locate an area for the hospital while there was still light to do so.

While Russell was out looking for a site for the hospital for the miners, the shoring for the mine excavation gave way, killing one of the mine owners and many of the guests. They brought Malachi to conduct a service for the mineworkers. Ricardo realized that the white, shiny Volkswagen was out of place with the ragged, dirty miners, and he had two miners shovel dirt all over Malachi. The miners said, "Now Malachi is one of us." Rival mining factions who had been killing each other came together for the meeting in which over 20,000 miners attended.

Another notable meeting during this time was with the National Police. Ricardo was invited to give hour-long messages for one week to police Special Forces training program. I was invited to tag along. Ricardo developed a beautiful method of bringing Christian conviction and new dedication to these police officers and non-coms. These were 40 of the best men the National Police had. Ricardo innocently asked, "How many of you have kept your oath of office since you joined the police until now?" As Ricardo knew, no one could raise his hand. This was very humbling to these proud officers. Ricardo then preached an hour-long Biblical message. At the end instead of an altar call, Ricardo challenged the men to retake their oath of office. This oath was full of good things they were supposed to be doing, summing up with 'For God and Country.' The officers were inspired to keep their oaths of office with God's help.

Later that week at a police checkpoint, a notorious drug lord was passing through. Even though there was an order for his capture, no one ever stopped him because he would have had them killed. The police captain at the checkpoint had been in Ricardo's class. The captain said, "Get out of the car. You are under arrest." The drug lord, said to one of his men, (he had three carloads of men with him,) "Give this man some money." When the captain refused it, the outlaw couldn't believe his ears.

"Give him some more money."

The captain said, "I am taking you in to show my respect for 'God and country.' You are under arrest."

A newspaper correspondent heard about the story and wrote it up in large type for the main Bogota newspaper, *El Tiempo*. The headline read, FOR GOD AND COUNTRY. The drug lord was able to get out by bribing a corrupt judge, but the tide was changing.

When Pablo Escobar had three out of six presidential candidates assassinated, President Barco laid his hands on the casket of his old friend Galan and said, "We're taking this country back from the drug traffickers. They put 20,000 men on the trail of Pablo Escobar for months and finally killed him. Gacha was killed just before that on the north coast.

Chapter VIII

Silent City

Walking in the Spirit in
COLOMBIA

A young man looked me up when I was in Bogota. His name was Bernie Hale, and he was a missionary to the deaf. He said there were several hundred deaf people in Bogota. He had worked out a system by which in six months he could teach them to communicate by sign language and shortly after that, lead them to the Lord. "Everyone I talk to says you are the man I should see," he told me. "Deaf people are happier if they marry other deaf people, and their dream is to have a community of their own. I have tried everywhere to obtain land, but it is all too expensive. Can you help us?"

This is how *Ciudad Silencio* (Silent City) began. I homesteaded a large tract of beautiful land, part open savannah and part jungle. Once I had the land registered and all the paper work done, I turned the land over to Bernie. He sent dozens of deaf people out there to construct *Ciudad Silencio* (Silent City). Chaddy came over to help them select the good trees for building from the jungle and supervise things.

Bernie was a terrible fundraiser, but finally he got together $4,000 dollars for a portable saw mill. The deaf people were very happy with their very own community and soon had a dining hall and their own food planted. They began raising pigs, but they had a problem with a big anaconda that lived in the adjacent stream, *Caño Jabón*. The deaf people couldn't hear the pigs scream when the anaconda grabbed them. Bernie sent out dogs with the hope that the dogs could alert the deaf folks when the anaconda came to get the pigs. However, the crafty anaconda ate the dogs. Finally we got the anaconda killed before he grabbed one of the children.

Bernie wasn't any too good at raising funds in the States, but what he did do was enlist a couple of dozen American young people to come down and help. They had no idea what they were getting into. One day in San Martin, over a dozen young people appeared at our house on their way to Silent City. They were all men or hardy looking women except for two frail looking girls in their early twenties. We sent the rest in the back of a dump truck where they had to stand up for over 19 hours bumping along a rough unpaved road. They then had to proceed for over an hour in a river launch.

I decided to fly the two frail women out to Silent City in our plane since I didn't think they could take the hard trip overland. *Ciudad Silencio* had its own airstrip. It was a little muddy, but I probably could have gotten the plane in there, but then I had a better idea. Chaddy hardly ever got to see any American girls, and I decided to land at *Chaparral* and have Chaddy take the girls by dugout canoe over to Silent City. They were very American-looking girls and I thought that at least one was reasonably attractive.

It was just at dusk when I landed at *Chaparral*. I said to Chaddy, "Find a place for these girls to sleep and take them over to *Ciudad Silencio* in the morning."

"I will be all tied up tomorrow," Chaddy replied, "They will have to go tonight."

A stream about 35-foot wide winds its way from the airstrip to the *Guaviari* River. We put the two girls into a dugout canoe with Armando at one end, and Chaddy with a 40 H.P. outboard motor at the back. With a tremendous acceleration, the girls disappeared from my sight. Chaddy always ran the motor at full throttle. Armando would call out to Chaddy when there was a submerged log, and Chaddy would raise the outboard to clear it without slowing down. The trees of the jungle covered overhead, and even in the daytime, that stream was dark. Both Armando and Chaddy held flashlights in their mouths.

I'm sure the poor girls were scared out of their wits. I was at the dock when Armando and Chaddy returned a few hours later. I overheard Chaddy saying to Armando, "Did you ever see two such homely girls in your life?" So much for my attempt at matchmaking.

Ciudad Silencio went on for many years, and the deaf lived out their dream of having their own community. We helped them all we could. It finally closed down when the guerrillas took over the area, although there might be a few of the deaf people out there yet. Bernie Hale now lives in Florida and continues to minister to the deaf in Bogota.

Chapter

IX

Refuges in Times of Need

Russell received an invitation from several churches in Peru to hold meetings there. He had an old car that was a pile of junk. It was a French Renault 4, which is probably the worst excuse for a car I have ever seen. However Russell was all happy with it and decided to drive it to Peru. I said, "Russell, fly down. Not only is the car not likely to make it, but part of the route is controlled by the M-19 guerrillas."

However Russell decided to drive down in his old bucket of bolts. "Give me a call when you break down, and I will send you the parts," I told him. Sure enough, I got a call from Popayan. He had broken down. What I didn't realize, however, was that God had a plan in mind. A Christian family took Russell in. They had a beautiful daughter who was living in a worldly manner, singing in a night club. Russell's hosts decided to take him to the nightclub to talk to their daughter and hear her sing. Colombian night clubs are extremely loud, and as the daughter came over to the table, Russell didn't know what to say, but the Lord helped him. "I can see that you are very talented, but are you happy?" he shouted in her ear over all the noise. This brought conviction to the young girl and reunited her with her family amidst repentance and tears.

Russell's host introduced him to the commanding officer of the local army battalion. This army colonel had been recently converted and became concerned for the spiritual condition of his troops. This battalion had suffered many loses and had been badly shot up by the M-19 guerrillas that were operating in the area.

The colonel lined up the whole unit and had Russell present the Gospel to them. After explaining everything he could, Russell decided to give an altar call by asking each soldier who wanted to commit his life to the Lord to take one pace forward. To Russell's amazement, every soldier there stepped forward. Russell thought that they must have misunderstood, so he went through the whole presentation again. Once again, everyone responded. From that date on, that unit did not suffer any more casualties. Six months later the guerrilla group that was fighting them, the M-19, decided that they didn't have the support of the people and signed a peace treaty with the government, becoming a political party instead of a guerrilla movement.

From the Sierra Nevada of Santa Marta, we got word that the Kogis were suffering an epidemic that I believe was due to fulminating, bloody bacillary dysentery. We were in San Martin, four hours away by light plane. However we were hindered from leaving for the mountains because our oldest daughter, Sharon had dengue fever. This is a very uncomfortable disease sometimes called 'break-bone fever.' Sharon is a registered nurse, and we really needed to have her with us. Sharon was soaking her hands and feet in ice water because of the intense itching that dengue fever brings. The urgency of the Kogi situation was upon us. I decided to lay hands on Sharon for her recovery. I said, "Sharon, the Lord lives in me, and I want you to believe that these hands are the Lord's hands. I laid my hands on Sharon in faith, and she instantly recovered. Fever, pain, and itching were all gone.

We got the plane ready for the four-hour flight over the 14,000 foot peaks of the Andes. The plane was to shuttle medicine and supplies out of an old spray plane field at Cienega about 30 miles south of Santa Marta. Complicating the whole operation was the news that the guerrillas were in the area of our airstrip at Mamarongo. Russell would have to carefully inspect the area for guerrillas. This all seems very hazardous, but I knew this epidemic could wipe out half the village. While I was buying supplies in Santa Marta, Russell was flying Patty and Sharon and cases of ampicillin into Mamarongo. We were on a very tight schedule because the plane license was due to expire the next day and had to be back in the *llanos* for an inspection. I got delayed in Santa Marta and arrived 10 minutes after the plane had taken off for the *llanos*. I couldn't believe it! I now had my family in Mamarongo, and I was still in Cienega. Mamarongo must have been free from guerrillas or Russell would not have landed there. However it was very likely the guerrillas controlled the trail between Mamarongo and the hot country below. My family and the Kogis needed me in Mamarongo, but I was too scared to go.

Meanwhile back in Mamarongo, almost every household had someone very sick. They watched the arrival of the plane from the ridges where they lived, and soon the airstrip was full of sick people. Sharon and Patty were so busy with the epidemic, they didn't have time to worry about what had happened to me. In the face of the epidemic, the guerrillas left Mamarongo for a different area. Sharon and Patty prayed for each sick Kogi and gave them medicine. From the time they arrived, no more Kogis died. The epidemic was stopped.

Back in Cienega, I was fasting and praying, trying to obtain the courage to go over the difficult trail to Mamarongo. I went to see an old missionary friend in Santa Marta. We prayed together for three days, until God gave me the courage to go. I put on an old cap to hide my blond hair and took a jeep to Palmor where the trail started. Palmor was a guerrilla-controlled town. I moved quickly through the town, trying to look inconspicuous. Four men standing in front of a store seemed to notice me. Soon I was on the trail, moving as fast as possible. I reached the river where my friend and coworker, Salomon was later shot and killed. Here I knew of a little-used trail that left the main trail and rejoined it high above. I knew I could run into guerrillas at any moment, but I hoped they would be on the main trail, not on this side trail. I was very pleased to cross the last ridge and look down on our house, the Kogi village, and the airstrip. Patty and Sharon were delighted to see me. Patty said, "Guess what, an army patrol came over that trail yesterday and are here in Mamarongo now. I praised the Lord that he had sent 22 soldiers ahead of me to make sure I wasn't ambushed. God has been looking after us for the full 38 years we have served Him in Colombia.

One of Russell's return flights to southeastern Colombia from Mamarongo shows God's special care for us and the airplane. Russell decided to cross the Andes farther north than usual. He couldn't get the plane much above 15,000 feet because ice was forming on the wings and there were mountains almost this high along his route with peaks up to 18,000 feet a few miles to his right. The weather was all socked in. After flying a long time, he should have flown past the Andes and be over the flat country of eastern Colombia. He was about to let down in the blind when he remembered the advice of George DeVoucalla, a veteran Wycliffe pilot, "Don't ever let down in the blind."

Russell found a little hole in the clouds and dived through. He came out in a rugged jungle-covered valley. Somehow he was still in the mountains. The valley had a little V shaped exit that was open. He flew through it and found a fine paved airstrip under him. He landed and asked the airstrip attendant the question every pilot dreads to ask, "Where am I?"

"This is Sogamoso," the man answered.

"There isn't any airstrip on the map here," said Russell.

"There is now," the man replied.

Because of the tremendous headwind of over 100 miles per hour, the government had rebuilt an abandoned strip complete with control tower there in case anyone needed it. "Yours is the first light plane I have seen in months," the man told him. As I said, the Lord looks after us. All we have to do is make sure we are walking in the Spirit and obedient to Him, and He takes miraculous care of us, according to His great power.

Chapter
X

In The
Nick
of Time

Walking in the Spirit in
COLOMBIA

I want to include the story of the conversion of my father at 91 years of age as an encouragement to those of you who have loved ones who are not saved.

My father and mother were not Christians, although my grandparents on my mother's side were wonderful Christians, and my grandmother prayed for me every day of my life until she died at the age of 96. My mother came to the United States to escape the strict environment of her Christian home. In her late eighties, she remembered her Christian upbringing and turned to the Lord.

My parents retired and moved to Florida. They saved their money and every three months, they went on a cruise. They got used to the fancy free drinks on the cruise ships and soon began making these drinks at home. Little by little, they became alcoholics. This changed the whole character of my father's personality, and he became ornery and insulting whenever I was in the house. He would bawl me out about the same dozen complaints he had against me as I was growing up. Over and over, like a broken record, it went. He also had complaints about his mother and sister who were no longer alive. He was drinking a whole bottle of whiskey a day at this point. Every day he repeated with tears the complaints about the time his mother had abandoned him in Montana when he was sixteen, and how his sister had gotten the lion's share of the inheritance.

I continued to pray for him, but it was an extremely difficult situation. Finally all his drinking caught up with him, and he began to lose strength. It was clear that he was dying. I was sent for and accompanied him at his bedside. He would have times of clarity for 10 or 15 minutes and then lapse into unconsciousness.

In one of his rational times I said to him, "Dad, we've got to get you safely to the other side of death to be with the Lord." I really didn't know what to do or say. Obviously this was not the time or place to present the six points of salvation. I earnestly prayed for guidance, and the Lord showed me he needed to forgive his mother, sister, and me. "Dad, you've got to forgive your mother for leaving you in Montana and your sister for hogging the inheritance, and whatever you have against me."

The Lord opened his eyes and understanding, and he earnestly forgave everyone for what he had against them. Then I said, "Now you can ask the Lord for your own forgiveness. He did so, and a great peace came over him, and the Lord saved him. He was grateful to me for interceding for him and said, "Thank you." He lived another two weeks, and he was a changed man. His half full bottle of whiskey on the table was never used again.

Verses on forgiveness:

. . . *and set us free from our debts, as we set free our debtors.*

. . . *For if ye set men free from their trespasses, your heavenly Father will also set you free: but if ye do not set men free from their trespasses, neither will your heavenly Father set you free from your trespasses.*
Matthew 6: 12, 14, 15.

. . . *And his lord was wroth and delivered him to the tormentors until he should pay all that was due unto him. So likewise shall my heavenly Father do also unto you unless from your hearts ye forgive every one his brother their trespasses.* Matthew 18:34,35.

Chapter XI

Through Wind, Rain, and High Water

One of my favorite people that I worked with in Colombia was Larry Devilbus, the missionary for Gospel Recordings. This mission would make short messages in tribal languages using bilingual Indians. Then the tribal missionary would distribute the records together with a little portable phonograph. I have a joke for you about phonographs. The old white haired missionary was going through customs, and the customs officer asked him, "Do you have any pornographic material with you. The old missionary replied, "Oh, no! Why I don't even own a pornograph."

Larry and I decided to travel together. Part of my job as tribal and technical studies coordinator for the Wycliffe Bible Translators was to survey and list the remaining tribes that needed translation. First we tried to locate the Machagenda Tribe and finally found them. They had lost their land and were living along side a river on a farm that wasn't theirs. They were malnourished and in sad shape. About 350 of them remained. I took down a word list for comparison purposes, but I knew that there were probably too few of them to warrant a translation of the New Testament. Larry did a set of gospel recordings for them.

Then we heard of an isolated tribe that few people had contacted. Living in a remote area and not wanting contact with other people, we realized this would be a real challenge. Just as we were praying and making big plans, someone told us that four of these Indians were in the local jail for murder. We got permission to visit these Indians in the prison yard. The yard was full of very tough criminals. It was too noisy to work linguistically, besides the other inmates were trying to scare us. One tough young man had made a wooden knife with a very sharp point. He suddenly whipped around and put the knife in my stomach, stopping just short of drawing blood. I said, "What did you do that for?" He replied that he had to keep his reflexes in shape for when he got out of jail.

Finally the Lord gave me a solution. I decided to rent two prison cells, one for me to take down a word list, and the other for Larry to make gospel recordings. I used a standard 450-word list of the most common words. With this list we could tell if one language was related to another and how close they were. We discovered that the group represented by the men in jail was quite close to the Cuivas where Wycliffe already had placed a team. We also found out the four Indians were innocent of murder. After the murder of a white colonist, the police had gone into their area and put in custody the first four Indians they could find. We prayed that the Lord would help us resolve all the problems and injustices we were discovering.

As we continued in our survey of Indian tribes in the department of Arauca, we came to the *Banadia* River. The water level was too low for the ferry to operate and too high to ford. But nothing was going to stop Larry. Larry marched out into the river, which was about 200 yards across and pronounced the river bottom solid. I couldn't believe he was going to try to ford this river which had trucks stopped on both sides because the drivers didn't think they could make it through. Larry disconnected the fan belt, and into the river we went.

At first it looked like Larry was going to make it, but right in the center of the river, we encountered a soft sand bottom. The wheels spun, and down we went. Larry really scrambled to save the very expensive sound recording equipment from getting wet. He borrowed a long chain and soon a truck pulled us out. I had a good laugh when Larry brought his suitcases out of the back end of the Land Rover with water running out of them. I thought my two suitcases were dry because they had been piled high in the back end. However when I opened them up, they were absolutely full of water. Now it was Larry's turn to laugh. My Bible was drenched. As I sat on a log drying the pages in the sun, a Colombian Christian came along and bawled me out to a fare you well. He was as mad as he could be. "You got the *Santa Biblia* (Holy Bible) all wet," he complained.

We could not go ahead, and we asked the Lord for direction when overhead flew a red twin aircraft. It was a twin Evangel of which there were only two in the country. Wycliffe had one, and a commercial operator had the other. We decided to go to the airport and see if anybody we knew was on the plane. I knew the plane owner, and he introduced me to the Governor of Arauca, who was on the plane. When the governor found out we worked with Indians, he was tremendously friendly and unusually interested. He was an amateur anthropologist, and information about Indians and their life-style was an obsession with him. He used the police and civil authorities of his department of Arauca to help him gather information about all the Indians in Arauca. He had a huge map of the department made, and on it he located all Indian groups in the department. The information was so detailed that in many cases he had long lists of the names of Indians in a certain location or tribal area. He duplicated the map for me. Obviously, such information was of tremendous help to Larry and me. On this map were groups that we didn't even know existed. There were extensions of tribes we were working with who were living in more accessible areas.

Now we could see the hand of the Lord in our direction. We had been prevented from crossing the *Banadia* River until the twin Evangel flew over with the governor aboard. We now had access to information that would have taken months to obtain. Surely the Lord was very interested that these tribes came to know Him and had worked out all the details. I told the Lord years ago, "You open the doors, and I'll walk through them."

The governor invited me to supper at the gubernatorial mansion. The invitation was for 7:00 p.m. Knowing that Colombian time is much later than the clock indicates, I thought I should arrive at about 8:30 p.m. However, then I remembered that this man had been trained in France, and maybe 7:00 p.m. meant 7:00 p.m. I knocked on the door of the imposing mansion at 7:00 p.m. Bad idea! After a while the door opened, and there stood the governor all confused in his underwear. "Go sit in the park for an hour, and then come back," he said.

At a little after 8:00 p.m. I knocked on the door again. This time I was kindly received as though nothing had happened. We had long talks about Indian policy. I told him about the four Indians in jail for a murder they did not commit. He called up the jail authorities and had them released.

Larry and I decided to visit the Cuiva tribe at the eastern end of Arauca. The terrain changed, and soon we were in heavy jungle. Larry had a little, skimpy inflatable rubber raft with which we crossed the river with fear and trembling. Two single lady linguists were working with the isolated tribe and were happy to have some visitors. One of them told me how this nomadic tribe functioned. I had visited other nomadic tribes, but this one was particularly ornery.

Nomadic jungle tribes stay in a given area for a week to several months, depending on how much wild game is available. The men are quite lazy and slept and fooled around after the game got scarce instead of going to the work of moving and setting up in a new area. Soon the women and children were crying with hunger. This didn't inspire the men any. It wasn't until the men got weak with hunger, and they realized that if they didn't move, they soon would be unable to do so.

There was no law and order in this little band of about 45 Indians. One man got mad at another and shot him in the stomach with an arrow. So much for the myth of the angelic life of a jungle Indian tribe. The women missionaries have done a wonderful job, and now there are many Christians with transformed lives.

Larry decided it was time to go to Bogota. The only problem was that someone had come over the wall of the missionary's house where we stayed and stole our windshield. This was not a big problem so long as it didn't rain. Coming into the town of *Codazzi*, a black line of ominous clouds lay ahead of us. It was already about 10:00 p.m., and the lightning ahead of us was awesome. I said, "Larry, lets find some porch where we can swing our hammocks and spend the night here."

"It's only a little storm," replied Larry, "I think I can see right through it." Larry never stopped to sleep or rest on a trip but pushed straight ahead. Soon the rain was so heavy that you couldn't see the front of the vehicle. We had a poncho, but it wasn't much help with the rain coming through the place where the front windshield used to be.

Finally all the water flooded out the engine. We were in the middle of nowhere. Through the heavy rain, I could just barely make out the outline of a house about 75 feet off the road. The people in the house were happy to allow us to tie up our hammocks in the house. It was a new house, which was extremely fortunate because an old house would have been full of cochroaches and parasites of every kind. I always marveled at how the Lord took care of Larry, even when he was stretching faith into presumption. I guess the Lord honored Larry's zeal.

In the night Larry got up to go outside and came in all excited. "Close the door, I think we have a baby danta inside. A danta is a large jungle animal. It turned out to be another animal that was a pet of the house owner. I just got back to sleep when before it was even light, Larry was up saying, "That's enough sleep. Let's get going."

I have selected many answers to prayer and direct leadings of the Lord to encourage believers to make a total commitment to the Lord and watch the Holy Spirit work in their lives in power as He has in the last 57 years that I have served Him.

Chapter XII

A Ray of Hope

Walking in the Spirit in
COLOMBIA

The Kogi Indian work has been extremely difficult. Orlando Corwin was the first missionary to try to work with the Kogis. He and his wife spent 14 years living just outside the Kogi area and never was able to spend even one night in a Kogi village or receive any help whatsoever with the language. It is a crime punishable by death for a Kogi Indian to give out language or cultural information. It was a great miracle for us just to be allowed to live with one Kogi family for two years, learning the culture and studying the very complex language. Then the Lord instantaneously healed the main chief and shaman of the Kogi village of Mamarongo when he was dying. This event gave us access to live in this village for many years. We daily treated and prayed for a number of sick Kogis, and they all recovered.

When Kogis walked for miles to see us, they were too skinny, weak, and malnourished to return home without nourishment. They would bring a hand of platanos or yucca, or something to eat with them in a big, loosely knit bag hanging from a head strap across their foreheads and give it to us. According to Kogi custom, when you do that, your name is in the pot for lunch. Everyday Patty would prepare a big kettle of food, throwing in everything available. The hardest part of this cooking was peeling all the vegetables, and the fact that all this was being cooked over a wood fire on the floor in a corner of our kitchen. Patty asked the tribal leadership to assign some woman to help. They said it was not their custom to have a woman work outside her family. However shortly after this, one of the tribal leaders came with his little, tiny daughter and said she would be willing to help Patty. I had to build a stool so she could reach the dishpan on the kitchen table. Her name was Mariana, and it turned out that she was a lot of help to Patty. She was probably not as young as she looked. She must have been eight or nine at the time, as she was the oldest of a whole string of younger sisters. She was excellent at keeping track of three-year-old Gloria, and keeping the fire going by adding sticks.

The spiritual work was slow and difficult. The few professions of faith were not accompanied with real spiritual life. We started a school, but nobody was able to learn to read. Our Wycliffe literacy expert said that because of the extreme protein deficiency in the tribe, we would have to improve the Kogi diet and await the next generation to teach them to read. We did our best to upgrade the Kogi diet. Patty began giving milk from the sacks of powdered milk we brought in to all the children who lived close to us. I brought in seeds. When we arrived, the Kogis were eating two small meals a day of boiled cooking bananas and yucca. I remember Kogi men sitting in our kitchen marveling at all the different things Patty could cook. One said to the others, "That Chad is so lucky. He gets something delicious to eat every meal." There were also other cultural problems. The Kogis had to have permission from the spirit world to plant or do anything. After the healing of the Kogi chief, Mama Nacio, I was considered a Kogi chief, and they took my admonitions to plant as permissions. We also brought in every kind of tool. They had only two old worn-out axes in the whole valley when we arrived. They were living in the Stone Age. The governor of the department of Magdalena pressured hardware stores in Santa Marta to give the tools. Also, the Indians were full of parasites, and we brought in case after case of medicine to cure round worm, hookworm, amebas etc. The Kogis were pygmies with men under 5 feet and women under 4 ½ feet due to the many factors I just mentioned.

The Kogis thought that I had a pill for everything. They wanted pills to make their skinny little wives fat. Most of all they wanted 'nice' pills that would make their ornery wives easy to get along with as they could see how nice Patty was. One Kogi man asked me, "When do you hit Patty with a piece of firewood to make her mind? We have been watching to see the black charcoal marks on her head, indicating a bang with firewood, but we haven't seen any. Everyone knows that women do not work and obey well unless you hit them over the head once in awhile with a piece of firewood."

I decided to use this occasion to present the Gospel. I said, "Patty was not always as good tempered as you see her now. She was really ornery until she presented her life to the Lord, and He changed her."

The Kogi man looked incredulous. "Maybe God could change a man, but a woman? Never!"

The Kogis had a cultural block to learning to read. They believed that years ago their people knew how to read, but that they had traded that ability for the right to use metal tools. It took Alfonso, our language helper five years to overcome this mental block and learn to read. Both he and Mariana became like members of our family. Mariana became the first true believer in the tribe, and I baptized her. We had worked twelve years and had only one believer to show for it. Mariana encouraged her family in the Lord. When we would show life of Christ films, (we had twelve 30 minute films) she saw to it that as many family members as possible were present. She could understand Spanish, and she explained the films to the people in the Kogi language.

Wycliffe asked us if two young ladies could help in the Kogi work. Linda Gawthorne and Bonny Brobston began working with the Kogis. Grace Henserling also joined them. Later on it became necessary for Linda to live in Bogota because of health reasons. She found a large house in Bogota and carefully selected Kogi boys to live with her in Bogota and receive an education. Of the ones selected, two were Mariana's sons and two were her younger brothers, about the same ages as her sons. These young men were very carefully raised by Linda Gawthorne in Bogota. The Lord must have given her much wisdom as each one has not only maintained his Kogi culture but also has become a strong Christian.

When they finished their education and returned to their tribal village, they established a flourishing school, as well as Christian meetings. Each young man had his own small coffee farm to meet his family's personal expenses. (I had taught the Kogis to raise coffee, the cash crop of the area, back in the '70's.) Most of them married. All was going very well. It seems that Satan could not let this success among the Kogis move ahead unhindered, and the guerrillas moved into the area. They closed down the school and burnt the houses belonging to the Christian Kogis. The Christians were given a choice: Either return to the old Kogi religion or leave the area. All of the Christians stood firm, and refused to deny the Lord.

Months later, one young man came to us and told his story:

After he and his family were forced to flee from their village, he was chosen as the family representative to go to the political leader of the Kogi village to seek aid in finding a place to relocate. The leader offered to help him and his family to establish themselves in a different area but said that they would have to renounce Christianity first. "Give me your answer right now," the leader told him. "Return to the traditional Kogi religion, and I will give you and your family all my support and find you a new place to live, but if you persist in Christianity, I will not help you. My own life would be in danger from the armed groups, if I gave help to Christians."

"I have no trouble giving you my answer," responded the young man. "I made my decision before, with a sub-machine gun pointing at my stomach. I have been a Christian for ten years, and I'm not going to deny the Lord now."

Then he told us what had happened the day the guerrillas came to his mountain home. The guerrilla leader had ordered him at gunpoint to renounce Christianity immediately. It was 12:00 noon, and suddenly the heavens let loose with a tropical downpour. Everyone was sent to seek shelter and ordered to gather again at 2:00 p.m. in the men's council house in the village. As he sat alone in his little house for two hours, the young Christian pondered his situation. An old Kogi man came by and counseled him to say whatever he had to say to save his life, in spite of his true feelings. As he prayed, the Lord was very near and precious to him. He realized that if the guerrillas shot him, he would go immediately to be with the Lord. On the other hand, if he renounced Christianity to save his life, his future would not be worth living.

At 2:00 p.m. they all gathered in the council house, and a guerrilla asked him for his answer. He told them that he would not renounce Christianity. The guerrilla started asking him other questions, but suddenly the leader of the 19th guerrilla front spoke up from back in the shadows. "Don't question him any further," he ordered, "We have all heard the young man's answer. I have given the order many times to shoot Christians (in the neighboring Arhuaco tribe), but I'm not going to do it this time. Let the young man go!" As our young friend gave us this testimony, his face shined with the glory and peace of the Lord. I'm sure even the hardened guerrilla leader was impacted by his sincerity and courage. None of the Christians were killed, even though their houses were burned down and their possessions destroyed.

The Christians numbered around forty—men, women, and children, and they had nowhere to go. Finally the government allowed them to stay for three months in a national park that contained a few Kogi houses as a tourist attraction. Several churches in Bogota took up offerings for them, and they were able to buy a fine piece of land outside the Kogi reserve and away from guerrilla control. They hold their own meetings and are raising their own food. They are fixing up a building in which to hold a school. Several boys from other villages are joining them to go to school. They just baptized seven more people. They hope to attract students from all over the Kogi tribe.

For years I wondered why the early church lived in

community. The Lord showed me that living in community is an excellent way to be perfected and conformed to the image of the Lord Jesus Christ. Once the Lord had the church in Jerusalem living in harmony and growing in grace, He did not leave them together to enjoy the fellowship but allowed a severe persecution to come and . . . *they went everywhere preaching the Gospel.* Acts 8:4

It appears that the Lord is doing the same with the Kogi believers. Their new farm is just below the Kogi reserve and is cool with good streams and plentiful water. Please pray for this work. It has been very hard, but now the guerrillas are breaking up the old spiritual customs. Three Kogi Mamas (religious leaders) have said that they no longer believe in their spirit world, as their gods were unable to keep the guerrillas out of their villages. This will result in a spiritual vacuum. After all this, we may yet see a real turning to the Lord among the Kogis.

Who would have imagined that little Mariana and some of the children to whom we fed milk and good nourishing food would become strong Christian leaders with a desire to see the Kogi tribe turn to the Lord. This is an ongoing work. The Kogi Christians will need overcoming prayer and financial help for years to come to enable them to fulfill their vision. An urgent need is money to purchase more land to raise more food. At the end of this book, you will see how you can help.

Chapter XIII

Ray Rising

Al Meehan, the director of the Wycliffe Bible Translators, came to my father's house in southern Florida. Al was an old friend and a pilot. He had flown us into the Kogi tribe many times, "Chad," he said, "We need your help with the kidnapping of Ray Rising. We have no contact with which to negotiate, and we don't know if Ray is alive or dead."

Ray Rising was the radioman for Wycliffe and a close personal friend. Many times, he had fixed the radios on our planes. At Lomalinda he had been a favorite youth leader of both Russell and Chaddy as well as a great encouragement to many of the local people. "We will certainly do all we can," I replied.

Chaddy asked the guerrilla leaders we had made contact with during Russell's kidnapping whether Ray was alive or dead. They said he was dead. We knew that the guerrillas often say that to get government agencies to drop the case. Sure enough, after a while they sent word to Chaddy that they wanted to negotiate.

Complicating the whole thing was that Wycliffe had a crisis committee to handle the kidnapping. A committee is difficult to negotiate with. I am reminded of the joke that a camel is a horse designed by a committee. The committee couldn't agree among themselves and angered the guerrillas by their delays and inept pronouncements. Wycliffe is an Indian mission that has very little to do with Spanish-speaking Colombians. Many members could not speak Spanish. As all these misunderstandings went on, Chaddy had to take the communications deep into the jungle to the guerrilla commander. Things became so confused and misunderstood that Chaddy had to make more than 20 trips, crossing two rivers and completely wearing out a Honda trail bike in the mud. Also, since this area was a war zone between the right wing paramilitary and the guerrillas, a half a dozen times, Chaddy came across wounded men on the trail and brought them to the hospital in Puerto Lleras.

Meanwhile at Lomalinda Russell maintained radio contact with Chaddy as he worked on his Spanish and English Bible translations. Wycliffe had shut down the base in the wake of Ray being kidnapped. The farm, Bonaire, and several of the houses were sold to us as the missionaries left and the rest was turned over to the government. Russell would mobilize the doctors at the local hospital in Puerto Lleras as Chaddy brought in the wounded.

One time Chaddy arrived at the guerrilla camp and found the commander so frustrated and angry at how the negotiations were going that he was in the act of issuing an order to kill every Wycliffe worker on sight. Chaddy calmed him down.

Finally the guerrillas told us, "We know you're not going to pay a ransom. Just give us the money that we have invested in this kidnapping, the food for Ray and his guards, and we will give you Ray Rising."

We couldn't get the crisis committee to agree to this, so Chaddy raised all the money he could, and I took out the rest on credit cards. We realized that if we didn't act fast, Ray would be killed. We went to see the Wycliffe director, but he wasn't there. He had left an acting director who was a reasonable man and a good friend. We explained we could get Ray out. He said, "Go get him." Later we were told the acting director didn't have authority to make that decision. We no longer cared! We had Ray Rising!

To see Ray's oldest son embrace his father after the two year absence was worth all the trouble we had. Ray wants to come back to Colombia and work on our radio station. Right now he is in radio maintenance with Christian radio in Bolivia.

Later on, Wycliffe helped us with a debt we had on the Finca Bonaire that we were purchasing from them.

Chapter XIV

Jubilee

From the time we entered Colombia in January 1964, we knew the available Scriptures in Spanish were sadly lacking in clarity and accuracy. About ten years ago, the Lord impressed on Russell to do something about it. We knew that there was an excellent old translation into Spanish done by Casidoro de Reina in 1569, but we couldn't find a copy in Colombia. Casiodoro was a contemporary of William Tyndale, and they knew each other. But Casiodoro had a great advantage as a Bible translator. He was fluent in Hebrew and understood all the Hebrew idioms whose meaning has been lost today. The Spanish Inquisition killed all the Jewish scholars they could find and made it impossible for Jews to openly speak Hebrew. This caused the Hebrew language to die out (scholars for many centuries studied Hebrew as a "dead" or unspoken language). This affected the meaning of all translations, English or Spanish or whatever resulting in many obscure areas. In our English translations for example, we find verses with a footnote saying, Hebrew idiom, meaning obscure.

We believe that in these last days when many Old Testament prophecies are being fulfilled, God wanted to make the Old Testament as clear as possible. We needed to find the old Casiodoro manuscript. Some friends were going to Spain, and we asked them to try to locate the manuscript. They were able to locate an exact copy recently republished to commemorate the reformation. I now have a copy, and it is beautifully done, like a pulpit Bible.

The sure sign that God was leading us came when we obtained a compact disk of an old revision of this translation. Now all Russell had to do was put the translation on one screen, and on another screen, he had a disk with 28 different translations. He began producing a revised translation, changing obsolete words and making all related terms consistent. It took him eight years, checking every verse of Casiodoro's translation against 28 translations, English and Spanish and against original Hebrew and Greek manuscripts. Since he was working on other projects in the daytime, he worked from 9 or 10 at night until 2 or 3 in the morning.

Not only is this wonderful Bible now finished, he applied all he learned to a new English translation as well. He just gave me a copy, bound in leather with my name on it. He calls it the *Jubilee Bible,* and you can order a copy of it or the Spanish Bible from my daughter, Gloria, in Florida.

When we looked for a publisher for Russell's first book, *Rescue the Captors,* and a Christian publisher made us a flattering offer, I heard one of their directors say to another, "We will take the material of the book and weave it around a theme that will sell." When Russell heard that, he turned them down. To us one of the great features of the book was that it was written from within a guerrilla camp. Whatever imperfections there were simply reflected the difficulties of living and writing among the guerrillas. The rough draft was part of the authenticity of the book. We decided to publish the book ourselves.

We found out that by filling out a form for the state, we could become a publishing house. That is how Ransom Press was born with the logo of a golden key. We now publish over 40 titles in both English and Spanish, specializing in books on holiness and a Godly life. All our titles are available from our daughter Gloria in Florida. The books are printed very cheaply in Colombia and shipped to Florida in a container.

Part of the beauty of this system is that all the profit above printing costs goes into our mission work. So, you can contribute to missions by buying one of our books. We have been heavily engaged in a literacy ministry and distributed over 100,000 books last year, books, not tracts. Our old friend, David Peacock, the printer at Buena Semilla in Bogota, gives us his books he can't sell. Usually they just have some minor flaw. Then they are distributed by all sorts of people, truck or taxi drivers, storekeepers, river launch captains all have been keeping a box of books available, and people are delighted to get a free book. We published a pocket New Testament with a camouflage cover for distribution to the guerrillas and the military. So far almost 30,000 copies have been given out.

When Russell returned from the United States about three years ago, a church had helped him obtain an FM transmitter. When he arrived in the *llanos*, he was unpacking the transmitter to test it out when he met an old friend who was a schoolteacher. The teacher asked if he had a license to operate it. Russell hadn't thought of that, but the teacher said that he and some community-minded friends had applied for and received one of the only five new licenses given out by the government that four year term. However they were soon going to lose the license because they had been given a year to get the station on the air but were unable to get a transmitter. As usual, the Lord was way ahead of us, and soon Radio Marfil Stereo 88.8 kHz was on the air 24 hour a day with good music, Christian messages and news. The beauty of our station is that it reaches under the dead spot that Bogota stations have because of the Andes and goes right into the main guerrilla controlled areas.

We have put up a beautiful 490-foot tower on the highest hill of Lomalinda, which we are rehabilitating. We have added an AM station and are working on a short wave station as well. Since the guerrillas keep knocking out power lines, we need a 75 K.W. generator and some other equipment that is available in the country for about $30,000. Anyone wishing to help with this or other needs of the station can send to the Pan-America Mission or Bethesda Fellowship in Canada. See instructions in the back of this book.

In Bogota we have sound studios and produce programs that are used all over Colombia.

In the next chapter I am going to share with you some of the most important information that I have researched during my many years in Colombia as a Bible translator.

Chapter XV

The Judgment Day

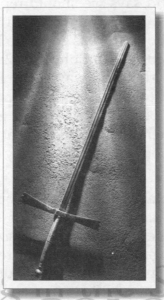

Walking in the Spirit in COLOMBIA

(How to Come Through It Victoriously)

To understand the final judgment and who is going to be judged we need to understand many doctrines that have been badly twisted today.

First of all we need to understand that when we use the famous verses of Ephesians 2:8, 9, &10, there is a contrast between 'works' in verse 9 and 'good works' in verse 10. When it says, "salvation is not of 'works'," it is talking about self works. Hebrews 6:1 calls them 'dead works,' and says we should repent from dead works. A dead work is any work that we have done, even those we thought were good. To be a true 'good work' in accordance with Ephesians 2:10, it has to be inspired by God, done His way and in His timing. Because of the great emphasis evangelicals have placed on the contrast between works and grace, we have missed the tremendous emphasis that the Scriptures place on true good works, initiated by God and done by us through His power.

To get some idea of the emphasis God places on true good works, let's look at the book of Titus. In three short chapters, the Holy Spirit emphasizes good works over and over again to the point of redundancy. In verse 1:16, Paul speaks of those who deny Him being abominable and disqualified for every good work. In chapter 2:7, Paul exhorts Titus to be a pattern of good works, and in verse 14, Paul states the purpose that Christ gave Himself for us was that He might redeem us from every lawless deed and purify for Himself His own special people, zealous for good works. In chapter three, Titus is told to remind the people to be ready for every good work. In 3:5, Paul states that Christ saved us, not by works of righteousness which we have done. By this he means religious works and dead works of every kind that we have done without His direction and power. In 3:8, Paul again states that Titus should affirm constantly that those who believed in God should be careful to maintain good works. After all these admonitions to good works, Paul closes the letter to Titus with the final admonition in 3:14, "Let our people learn to maintain good works, to meet urgent needs, that they may not be unfruitful."

One of the greatest contributors to the worldliness of the Church today is the lack of the fear of the Lord. "The fear of the Lord is the beginning of wisdom." (Proverbs 9:10) Just a few years ago, a Godly man was referred to as a God-fearing man. Not any more. The preaching of the superficial, easy-believism gospel has made millions of people think that because they have made a profession of faith, they have nothing to fear at the judgment day. But the Scriptures speaking to Christians say that every one of us will have to give an account of himself to God. "For we shall all stand before the judgment seat of Christ." (Romans 14:10) "So then, each of us shall give an account of himself to God." (Romans 14:12) These verses are clearly directed to Christians.

These warnings of a judgment day are all through the Scriptures written to Christians. Romans 2:6 says, "who will render to each one according to his deeds.

Eternal life to those who by patient continuance in <u>doing good</u> seek for glory, honor, and immortality." And speaks in v.16 of the day when God will judge the secrets of men by Jesus Christ according to my (Paul's) gospel.

To this agrees Romans 6:22, & 23, "But now having been set free from sin and having become slaves of God, you have your fruit to holiness, and the end eternal life. For the wages of sin is death, but the gift of God is eternal life in Jesus Christ our Lord." A similar verse casts more light on the subject. Galatians 6:8-10, "For he who sows to his flesh will of the flesh reap corruption, but he who sows to the Spirit will of the Spirit reap everlasting life. And let us not grow weary while doing good, for in due season we shall reap, if we do not lose heart. Therefore as we have opportunity, let us <u>do good</u> to all. . ." This eternal life as a free gift is not just the forgiveness of sins. The free gift is Christ Himself. He <u>is</u> Eternal Life. His communication with us through the Scripture and through the Living Word directing us is how this life is maintained, and John 6:63 tells us this is Eternal Life, itself.

Here and many other places in the Scriptures, we find eternal life as a final possession, the result of a lifetime of doing good. How can this be? Don't we receive eternal life the moment we believe? I am a linguist and Bible translator. The solution to this problem is that the word 'eternal' has two meanings in the Greek. One has to do with length and the other with quality. Usually the term, eternal life, has to do with quality, not length. Eternal life is another complete class of life. It is God's life, not just our human life prolonged forever. In Jude verse 7 we have Sodom and Gomorrah suffering eternal fire. That fire is not still burning. It was another class of fire, God's fire.

We do not have eternal life in ourselves. John 5:26 says, "For as the Father has life in Himself, so He has granted the Son to have life in Himself, but we have life only in the Son. (I John 5:11 &12) "And this is the testimony: that God has given us eternal life, and this life is in His Son. He who has the Son has life; he who does not have the Son of God does not have life." 'Have the Son' means to have Him in complete control as Lord. We do not have our glorified bodies yet; we have not yet put on incorruption. Only after a life of service to Christ, allowing Him to direct and empower us in every good work, will we inherit eternal life as a personal possession. This life can be short as the thief on the cross, or long as Polycarp, who stated before his martyrdom, "Eighty and six years have I served Him, and He has done me no wrong, how can I then blaspheme my king who has saved me?"

In Revelation 20:11-15 we have the great final description of the Judgment Day. "Then I saw a great white throne and Him who sat on it, from whose face the earth and the heaven fled away. And there was found no place for them. And I saw the dead, small and great, standing before God, and the books were opened. And another book was opened which is the book of life. And the dead were judged <u>according to their works</u> by the things which were written in the books. The sea gave up the dead who were in it, and death and Hades delivered up the dead who were in them. And they were judged each one <u>according to his works</u>. Then death and Hades were cast into the lake of fire. This is the second death. And anyone not found written in the Book of Life was cast into the lake of fire. Twice in this passage we are told that everyone will be judged by their works. For 19 hundred years the Church believed this to be true.

However in the last 80 years, a new teaching has come into the evangelical church. It holds that professing Christians can be guilty of gross immorality but will never come into judgment. Unbelievers, however, who do the same things will be condemned. Well, God shows no partiality. (Romans 2:11) Professing Christians will not get a special deal. Referring to Christians, it says that he that does wrong shall receive for the wrong he has done. (Colossians 3:25) Also, certain verses are taken out of context, such as Romans 8:1. "There is now no condemnation to those who are in Christ Jesus." They leave out the vital condition that follows, "who do not walk according to the flesh, but according to the Spirit." Some try to avoid this condition by saying that it is not in the oldest manuscripts, but it is repeated in verse 4. The condition of walking in the Spirit to avoid spiritual death is all through Romans 8. Romans 8:13 is one of the clearest, "If you live according to the flesh, you will die; but if by the Spirit, you put to death the deeds of the body, you will live."

How did the church ever get into such a difficult conflict? I believe it was when they wrongly identified what it meant to be saved by works; they never understood that <u>Christ in you</u> does the good works. This coupled with the wrong view of what Christ did for us set us up for this great contradiction as to whether believers would be judged. When the Scripture states that by the works of the law shall no flesh be justified, we assumed this to mean 'good works.' However the Bible never depreciates true good works. James 1:27 says, "Pure and undefiled religion before God and the Father is this: to visit orphans and widows in their trouble and to keep oneself unspotted from the world." Also in the Old Testament we find a universal truth. "He has shown you, O man, what is good; and what does the Lord require of you, but to do justly, to love mercy, and to walk humbly with your God?" Micah 7:8

This is enough to show that we have made a terrible mistake equating works of the law with good works, such as helping widows and orphans. This tremendous error has caused the evangelical church to be greatly deficient in good works, such as helping the needy. The early church was not so. Galatians 2:10 "They (the Jerusalem Church) desired only that we should remember the poor, the very thing which I was eager to do." It is interesting that when I began to walk in the Spirit, the Lord led me immediately into many good works. So what does the term, works of the law, stand for. In addition to self-originated works, both good and bad (dead works), I believe the works of the law were keeping religious observances such as circumcision, Sabbath keeping, various dietary restrictions, set fasting dates, ceremonial washings, etc. The works of the law certainly were not helping the poor etc. Going back to Ephesians 2:8, 9, 10, we have a contrast of 'works' verse 9 with 'good works' verse 10. These good works were so important for the new believer that the Scriptures make the strongest possible admonition in 2:10. "For we are His workmanship, created in Christ Jesus for <u>good</u> works, which God prepared beforehand that we should walk in them." God has prepared a whole series of good works for us to do, and indeed, we were specifically created in Christ Jesus for this purpose.

While we are on the subject of the Judgment Day, we need to address the problem of what will happen to unbelievers on that day. This subject has the potential to divide the church and cause bitterness. As a matter of fact, several of my fellow missionaries wanted to have me kicked out of the mission for my views on this subject until the mission discovered that about a third of the missionaries agreed with me, and that my views did not contradict the mission statement of faith. The doctrine that got everybody upset was concerning what would happen at the Judgment Day to people who had never heard the Gospel. They held that God would torture all these billions of people with conscious everlasting punishment with fire and brimstone. This would make God an unjust tyrant. If Hitler had tortured the Jews destined for the gas chamber with a day's torture or even an hour's torture before they died, it would have immensely aggravated the crime. To hold that God is going to torture people who have never heard for eternity is a doctrine that causes rational people everywhere to be revolted and not even listen to the Gospel. God greatly resents being presented as an unreasonable tyrant. I have walked with the Lord for 57 years, and I can sense His strong indignation for being presented as the worst tyrant by far of all time.

This brings us to consider the meaning of the word, 'perish.' "God is not willing that any should perish, but that all should come to repentance." (II Peter 3:9) Perish means total destruction from the presence of the Lord, which is forever without end. There is no second chance; no final reconciliation. Everyone will appear before the judgment seat of Christ. Those that have done wrong will receive a punishment commensurate with their crimes and the knowledge that they had. Everyone not found written in the Lamb's Book of Life shall be cast into the lake of fire which is the second death, the death of the soul. Since we know these things beforehand, what manner of men should we be? (II Peter 3:11)

We need to return to the example of John Bunyan's *Pilgrim's Progress* where Christian goes through many trials and temptations and finally arrives at the Celestial City. This story, which sold more copies than any other book except the Bible in its day, is an excellent example of the doctrine of final perseverance of the saints. It inspired whole generations of Godly people and played a vital roll in the Great Awakening. We have largely forgotten its teachings today, thinking that if we said the right words and accepted what Christ has done for us, that our spiritual journey is over, and no one can require anymore of us, or it would be trying to add works to grace. We have already shown that the Bible does not ask us to accept what He has done for us (a doctrine), but it asks us to accept Him (a person), and He comes only as Lord. It is not sufficient to believe that Christ died and rose again (even the devils believe this), but we must be identified in His death, so that the power of the Holy Spirit that raised Him from the dead might be active in us.

Let me summarize how I think the preaching of the Gospel and the life of the new believer are supposed to work. I have noticed that in just about all conversions, someone was earnestly praying for that person. The example of Charles Finney comes to mind. Two little old ladies came to him and asked if he minded if they prayed for him. He had been attending the local prayer meeting just because in that little town there wasn't much to do. He replied that they could pray for him, but he didn't think it would do much good as God hadn't answered any of the prayers of that little church in the two years he had been attending. In a little grove of trees, the power of God came with such force that Finney was on his knees under conviction for six hours. Finney began witnessing with the anointing of God for the rest of his life, and tens of thousands were converted. So the key is persistent, prevailing prayer, which then brings conviction. Soon God will bring that person under hearing of the Gospel. It has pleased God by the foolishness of preaching to save those that believe. (I Corinthians 1:21) It has to be of course anointed preaching, presenting the death and resurrection of Christ, not only as facts to be believed, but the convert must be identified in the death of Christ to receive pardon for sins, and be identified in the resurrection, so that the same power that raised Christ from the dead can raise up the new believer in newness of life. (Romans 8:11) The new believer must repent, confess, and turn from all known sin, identifying in Christ's death and then put faith and confidence in Christ to deliver him from the power of the sins he just confessed. This is what Paul taught publicly and from house to house. "Repentance toward God and faith towards our Lord Jesus." (Acts 20:21) Repentance and faith are also the first two fundamentals of the faith according to Hebrews 6:1,&2.

Once the new believer has availed himself of the Gospel, which is simply, "you dead, and Christ alive in you as your King," the believer is a candidate for water baptism. Baptismal regeneration is a great error espoused by many groups. But if your heart is right, and it is your desire to publicly identify in the death and resurrection of Jesus Christ, this will be the moment when the New Covenant is finalized, both for you and for God. When you make a contract with someone you can work out the details, but the contract is not valid until you sign it. We can think of baptism as the decision-making moment for the New Covenant. From that moment on, you agree to be crucified with Christ, and God promises to give you His Holy Spirit. "Then Peter said unto them, 'Repent and be baptized every one of you in the name of Christ for the remission of sins, and ye shall receive the gift of the Holy Spirit.'" (Acts 2:38) In every conversion in the New Testament, the new convert was baptized the same day. Obviously the disciples were using water baptism as the decision-making moment in their evangelism. This is especially clear in the conversion of the Philippian jailor. Wouldn't you think that after an earthquake, and with Paul and Silas hungry and with wounded backs from the stripes they had received that he would have waited until daylight for baptism? But Paul considered this so important that he accomplished the baptism that same night. The symbolism of the baptism is perfect to show our identification with Christ in His death and resurrection. Under the water, you can't breathe. It is cold there like the tomb, a perfect illustration of death. When you come out of the water, you can breathe again. This is a symbol of the resurrection. Now why did God put baptism right at the beginning of the Christian life? God wanted it perfectly clear right from the beginning that you are supposed to be dead (to your own way) and Christ alive in your body. It does not refer to the words used at the time of baptism.

In the early church, right after baptism the elders would lay hands on the new convert to be baptized in the Holy Spirit. The Lord would then give a spiritual gift or gifts. The words 'baptized in the name of Jesus' signifies becoming one person with Christ, being baptized right into Christ Jesus. The believer also became one person with all other believers (the body of Christ), the Church.

To maintain this intimate fellowship, the believer needs to 'walk in the Spirit.' Galatians 5:16, "Walk in the Spirit, and you shall not fulfill the desires of the flesh." The Lord showed me long before I came to Colombia that to 'walk in the Spirit' meant that all your decisions needed to be by the Spirit, even the smallest. The Lord will direct everything once everything is turned over to Him: your family, work or school, finances, leisure time, etc. He will direct where to read in the Bible and give understanding and power to carry out the Biblical demands. The Bible gives generalities and the Spirit gives specifics. The Bible tells us to love our neighbor but doesn't tell us for today which neighbor in what way. The Holy Spirit fills in the details and gives the power to carry it out. If all Christians would walk in the Spirit, we would save a lot of time doing things that are not really vital to the Kingdom of God.

There are many conditions to leading the Christian life. I will list just a few. If you do not forgive others, your sins cannot be forgiven. If during your Christian life, you refuse to pardon someone, your own pardon will be cancelled. (Matthew 6:14, 15 & 18:35) If we do not confess Christ before men, He will not confess us before the Father. (Luke 12:8) If these conditions offend you, be careful. Many are called, but few are chosen. (Matthew 20:16) II Peter 1:5-10 tells us to make our calling and election sure by adding to our faith virtue, knowledge, self-control, perseverance, godliness, brotherly kindness, and love.

Another condition is continuing in the faith: "If you continue in My word, then are ye my disciples indeed." (John 8:31) ". . . (they) persuaded them to continue in the grace of God." (Acts 13:43) ". . . and exhorting them to continue in the faith." (Acts 14:22) "If you continue in the faith, grounded and settled . . ." (Colossians 1:23) "Take heed unto thyself and unto the doctrine; continue in them for in so doing thou shalt both save thyself and them that hear thee." (I Timothy 4:16)

What happens to the Christian if he should sin or if God convicts him of some shortcoming in his life: Once again the Gospel comes into action. In Romans 1:16 Paul says he is not ashamed of the Gospel for it is the power of God unto salvation. Now 'salvation' in the Scriptures is always salvation from sin. The power of the death and resurrection of Christ must be applied to the sin. The believer must identify this sin in the death of Christ by confession, repentance, restitution, or apology, or whatever the Spirit indicates to be done, and then put faith and trust in Christ, not only to forgive the sin, but also to give the victory over it. The idea of superficially confessing sin, paying a little penance, and then committing the same sin in the immediate future makes a mockery of God's great salvation that He secured for us at such an enormous cost.

One of the most important things that the Scriptures teach us is how our sins are forgiven. First let me state two errors concerning this great truth. First, Christ did not suffer in Hades for our sins as some well-known teachers have taught. To have the demons stomping all over poor Jesus may make for sensational preaching, but it is not true. As one well-known teacher said after he renounced this doctrine, "When Christ said, 'It is finished,' He did not mean 'to be continued in hell.'" Christ descended into Hades as a Victor and set the captives free. He brought Abraham, Daniel, and the other heroes of the Old Testament up to heaven with Him.

The other outstanding error of how Christ paid for our sins is to misinterpret, "My God, My God, why hast thou forsaken Me?" If Christ were separated from God at that time, it would have been one of the most calamitous moments in all of history. The God head would be broken; the entire universe would go into chaos if Christ died spiritually. He not only created the universe, but He maintains the whole universe right now. (Colossians 1:16, 17) If He were separated from God, then how did He get back in fellowship again? In Luke 23:46 Jesus says, "Father, into Your hands I commit My spirit." He is in fellowship with the Father at this point and obviously still had His spirit.

Perhaps the most telling blow against the idea of God's turning His face from Christ when Jesus said, "My God, My God, why hast thou forsaken Me," comes from the 22nd Psalm itself. This Psalm begins with these words that Christ spoke on the cross and details Christ's sufferings—even to the casting of lots for His garments. In verse 24 of this Psalm depicting Christ's suffering on the cross, we find: "For He (God) has not despised nor abhorred the affliction of the afflicted, <u>nor has He (God) hidden His face from Him (Christ)</u>, but when He (Christ) cried to Him (God), He (God) heard." We find that God anticipated this error and made provision for correcting it in the Psalm itself.

Now it remains to be shown what the cry, "My God, My God, why hast thou forsaken Me?" really means. First of all, God does not take Jesus down from the cross, and in this sense He is forsaken. Also, He has to taste of death for every man. (Hebrews 2:9) When Christians die, they are absent from the body and are immediately present with the Lord. (II Corinthians 5:8) Our body dies, but our spirit goes right through death to be with the Lord, and there are many testimonies of Christians that received much comfort at their time of death. Some, such as Stephen, even saw the heavens opened and the Lord waiting for them. However, Christ tastes of death for every man and receives no physical succor nor help from God. No angel comes and attends to His thirst, for example. God forsakes Him as far as physical help is concerned, but to call this total separation from God and spiritual death is to push the meaning far beyond what actually occurred as recorded in the Scripture. Actually, God is strengthening Him in His Spirit as the Scripture tells us, "God was in Christ, reconciling the world unto Himself." (II Corinthians 5:19) Also, the 22nd Psalm in such verses as 21, "You have answered me," and verse 24, "But when He cried to Him, He heard."

The true atonement is based on our identification with Christ as our sacrifice. When Jesus died physically, He had His spirit still alive as He says to God, "Into Thy hands I commend My spirit." (Luke 23:46) Then after His resurrection He offers 'whosoever will' to become one person with Him in the Spirit, which means that when He died, so did we; when He arose, so did we; and then there's more: when He ascended to the Holy of Holies, so did we! (Hebrews 9:12 &10:19) If you are truly one person with Christ, then His death is your death and according to Romans 6:7, "he that has died is justified from sin." You can't bring a charge against a dead man. (Romans 8:33) "Who can bring a charge against God's elect? It is Christ who died." (and us with Him. Galatians 2:20) No judge will receive a charge against a dead man. The single death of the last Adam, the representative man, is sufficient to include all the sins of everyone who has become one person with Jesus Christ. Of course, if you do not wish to be crucified with Christ and live in His new resurrected life, there is no forgiveness of sins for you, and you will not be born again and given His Spirit.

Among the conditions to continue in the Christian life is expressed in Romans 8:17, "If we suffer with Him, we shall also reign with Him." Christ not only came to baptize us with the Holy Spirit, but also with fire. II

Timothy 3:12 tells us that "Those that live Godly in Christ Jesus <u>shall</u> (not may) suffer persecution." The trial of your faith refines your soul from impurities as we here in Colombia well know. We have lost 30 pastors and have had over 100 churches destroyed just in eastern Colombia where we have been working so many years. God is purifying the dross from His church.

"For this reason Christ died and rose again, that He might be Lord of both the living and the dead." (Romans 14:9)

"For the grace of God that brings salvation has appeared to all men, teaching us that, denying ungodliness and worldly lusts, we should live soberly, righteously, and godly in the present age, looking for the blessed hope and glorious appearing of our great God and Savior Jesus Christ, who gave Himself for us, that He might redeem us from every lawless deed and purify for Himself His own special people, zealous for <u>good works</u>." (Titus 2:11-14)

Witnessing therefore is based on Matthew 5:16, "Let your light so shine before men that they may see your <u>good works</u> and glorify your Father in heaven."

As I mentioned before, the superficial gospel has only been preached in the church to any great extent for the last 80 years. Jesus does have a church without spot or wrinkle. They are the overcomers and martyrs of all ages who are with Him right now around the throne, waiting until the full number is completed. (Revelation 6:9-11; 13:8:13-17) "Therefore we also, since we are surrounded by so great a cloud of witnesses, let us lay aside every weight, and the sin which so easily ensnares us, and let us run with endurance the race that is set before us." (Hebrews 12:1)

Conclusion

We need to follow the example of the apostle Paul when he says, "That I might know him (Christ), and the power of his resurrection, and the fellowship of his sufferings, being made conformable unto his death; If by any means I might attain unto the resurrection of the dead. Not as though I had already attained, either were already perfect . . ." Phil. 3:10-12

Not only has the 'easy believism,' superficial gospel of today resulted in lives indistinguishable from non-Christians (the Gallup Poll records just as many divorces, unwed mothers, and so forth in the church as in the population at large), far worse are the constant splits and scandals taking place in today's church. The average church member goes through three or four splits in his time attending church. After about four splits or serious problems, he withdraws from active church participation and either quits going to church altogether or joins a large or formal church where he can remain anonymous.

We need to return to the love and true good works of the New Testament: "Let your light so shine before men that they may see your good works and glorify your Father which is in heaven." Matt. 5:16; "By this shall all men know that ye are my disciples, if ye have love one to another." John 13:35; We need to return to the attitude of being ready to lay down our lives for each other that marked the early victorious church that overcame the Roman Empire.

Since that time , we have had many Godly men and movements. We need to return to these Godly examples.

Patty and I are writing a new book listing some of the great heroes of the faith and how they walked in the Spirit and overcame all obstacles. Since Bible times, the church has a list of heroes of the faith equal to the list of Old Testament saints in chapter 11 of Hebrews. I am including just one of these lives as an inspiration to today's Christians to become overcomers and attain to the prize of the high calling. "...I press toward the mark for the prize of the high calling of God in Christ Jesus." Phil. 3:14

In my opinion, the most important Christian worker we have had since the apostles was John Wesley. To him we owe such advances as the Sunday School which he held all Sunday long to teach reading and writing, arithmetic, history, and the Old and New Testaments to illiterate miners, farmers, and factory workers. The Methodists of John Wesley's day secured much better working conditions by forming unions. Eleven of the first twelve martyrs of the union movement were Methodists.

They also secured laws stopping the exploitation of child labor and extended their Sunday Schools to give daily education to poor children in a time when only the children of rich people were educated. Their schools spread all over the British Isles and were nationalized by the Crown with Wesley's permission. This became the first public school system in the world and was the model for the American and Canadian public schools of today.

Wesley and Whitfield revived the preaching of "you must be born again" and gave altar calls. Great conviction of sin followed and a great revival continued for over 150 years. Hundreds of thousands were brought into the Kingdom of God. No one was considered a Christian until God's Spirit witnessed to their spirit that they were born again, and their lives changed. They then proceeded to change the whole exploitive society in which they lived.

Just about every great social reform we enjoy today was begun at this time – orphanages, old people's homes, clinics and hospitals for the general populace, and prison reform. (Many prisoners were led to the Lord on their way to the gallows.) The music of Charles Wesley and his 6,000 hymns allowed the tremendous joy of these Christians to be expressed. "Why should the devil have all the good tunes?" asked Charles.

The worldwide thrust of Christian Missions went everywhere. "The world is my parish," said John Wesley. The elementary schools went on to add high schools and finally universities were begun. Harvard, Yale, Princeton and many other schools were founded in the late 1700's by great men of God, such as Timothy Dwight and Jonathan Edwards. Their main purpose was to prepare men for the ministry. A great move of God in the United States, called the Great Awakening, spread through the somewhat legalistic churches of the day. Tens of thousands had an intimate experience with God and transformed their communities for good. Open air preaching reached up to 30,000 at a time, and camp meetings with a great many people finding God were common. The thousands of circuit riding preachers discipled the converts and brought in new ones.

John Wesley was converted in 1738 and preached to ever-increasing crowds often four times a day. He rode tens of thousands of miles and lived to be 86 at which time there were 600,000 Methodists in the British Isles, all showing changed lives.

The leading of the Holy Spirit in these people was very evident. I will give some incidents from Wesley's daily journal to show God's hand on his ministry. He crossed the Irish Sea seven times. On his fifth proposed voyage, the Holy Spirit indicated to him to postpone the passage. The ship he was intending to take was lost in a great storm and sank. Everyone on board was lost.

On another occasion he woke up in a town that was experiencing a great fire. Everyone panicked. John said he never did anything without praying first. When he got up from his knees, he looked out the window, and the wind had changed, blowing the fire away from the building he was in. Drunken mobs and individuals many, many times tried to kill John. Now I am going to give you a remarkable incident of God's saving hand quoting directly from John's journal in his own words.

Friday, February 12, 1748 – "After preaching at Oakhill about noon, I rode to Shepton and found them all under a strange consternation. A mob, they said, was hired, prepared and made sufficiently drunk, in order to do all manner of mischief. I began preaching between four and five; none hindered or interrupted at all. We had a blessed opportunity, and the hearts of many were exceedingly comforted. I wondered what was become of the mob. But we were quickly informed: they mistook the place, imagining I should alight (as I used to do) at William Stone's house, and had summoned by drum all their forces together to meet me at my coming: but Mr. Swindells innocently carrying me to the other end of the town, they did not find their mistake till I had done preaching: so that the hindering this, which was one of their designs, was utterly disappointed. However, they attended us from the preaching house to William Stone's throwing dirt, stones, and clods in abundance; but they could not hurt us. Only Mr. Swindells had a little dirt on his coat, and I a few specks on my hat.

"After we were gone into the house, they began throwing great stones, in order to break the door. But perceiving this would require some time, they dropped that design for the present. They first broke all the tiles on the penthouse over the door and then poured in a shower of stones at the windows. One of their captains, in his great zeal, had followed us into the house and was now shut in with us. He did not like this and would fain have got out; but it was not possible; so he kept as close to me as he could, thinking himself safe when he was near me: but staying a little behind – when I went up two pair of stairs and stood close on one side, where we were a little sheltered – a large stone struck him on the forehead, and the blood spouted out like a stream. He cried out, "O sir, are we to die tonight? What must I do? What must I do?" I said, "Pray to God. He is able to deliver you from all danger." He took my advice and began praying in such a manner as he had scarcely done ever since he was born.

"Mr. Swindells and I then went to prayer; after which I told him, "We must not stay here; we must go down immediately." He said, "Sir, we cannot stir; you see how the stones fly about." I walked straight through the room and down the stairs; and not a stone came in, till we were at the bottom. The mob had just broken open the door when we came into the lower room; and exactly while they burst in at one door, we walked out at the other. Nor did one man take any notice of us, though we were within five yards of each other."

John preached daily. Until he was 80 he rode on horseback averaging 8,000 miles per year. After that, his friends got him a carriage, and he continued preaching until he was 86. England had been transformed. Now in the same places where drunken mobs had tried to kill him, people lined the streets with their hats in their hands just as though the King were passing by.

Afterward:

The books referred to in the text:
Rescue the Captors by Russell Stendal
The Guerrillas Have Taken Our Son by Chad and Pat Stendal
High Adventure in Colombia by Chad and Pat Stendal

Can be ordered from Ransom Press, International
        P.O. Box 400
        Moore Haven, FL 33471
        U. S. A.
        Tels: 863-902-3656 and 863-946-1776
        e-mail: bookorders@colombiaparacristo.com
                gstendal@aol.com

Tax-deductible receipts can be received for gifts to this on-going ministry.

In the United States:
        Pan-America Mission, Inc.
        P.O. Box 429
        Newberg, Oregon 97132-0429

In Canada:
        Bethesda Fellowship
        P.O. Box 21099 Ridge Post Office
        Maple Ridge, BC V2X 1P7

Gifts may be designated for the support of
_____ Chad & Pat Stendal
_____ Russell & Marina Stendal
_____ Chaddy & Yolanda Stendal

Special projects such as,
_____ Kogi ministry
_____ Radio ministry
_____ Bibles
_____ Literature ministry
_____ Displaced people

Web sites: www.colombiaparacristo.com (English)
              www.fuerzadepaz.com (Spanish)